10|23

Real Men Don't Rehearse

Real Men Don't Rehearse

Adventures in the Secret World of Professional Orchestras

by Justin Locke

Fifth Printing
Printed in the USA

Published by

Justin Locke Productions
Boston, Massachusetts

ISBN # 0-615-13029-1

www.justinlocke.com

Also by Justin Locke:

Principles of Applied Stupidity
(How to Get and Do More by
Thinking and Knowing Less)

Family Concert Works:

Peter VS. the Wolf
For orchestra and five actors; music by Prokofiev;
Published in USA by Justin Locke Productions.
Published in Europe by
Internationalen Musikverlagen Hans Sikorski.
Available in English, German,
Portugese, and Chinese versions.

The Phantom of the Orchestra
(or, the Dark Side of the Symphony)
(For orchestra and five actors;
Music by Bach, Mozart, Massenet,
Beethoven, et al.)

To read the scripts, and for information about renting these
programs for live performance, visit the Justin Locke
Productions Web site at www.justinlocke.com.

Well here it is, the fifth printing of *Real Men Don't Rehearse*. Who would have thought? The success of this book has been a dream come true for me, and I want to thank all the people who have purchased the book. I also want to thank all of those who have shared their kind comments with me.

I also want to thank the many people who have helped me in promoting it, including both those who have reviewed it and published excerpts, and those who have been kind enough to invite me to speak at their events and on their radio and television programs. Many thanks to Madeleine Crouch, and thanks also to Jen Hocko, who was has been responsible for innumerable overall improvements.

I would also like to thank Tom Treece, and it's also about time I said a thank you to my brother Joe, who long ago gave me a significant portion of his earnings from an after-school job washing dishes at a pizza parlor so I could buy my first string bass.

–JL

Introduction

There are many famous conductors and composers who are the stars in the world of classical music. You see their pictures on the covers of CD's, you see them interviewed on *60 Minutes*, and there are lots of books written about them. They have their roles to play, and they are important ones, but for all the hype surrounding these big names, the fact is, they aren't really the ones who are creating the music. Whether it's a pop ballad, a symphony by Beethoven, or the soundtrack of a major motion picture, the actual *sound* of an orchestra is created, note by note, not by these stars, but by individual orchestral musicians.

Professional orchestral musicians live in a secret society that is seldom seen by outsiders. Even when an orchestra is in full view of an audience, their world is largely invisible. This is not an accident. Even though they are in "show business," most orchestral musicians are rather shy and introverted people. Also, the people who market classical music assume that the audience is only interested in the stars and the glamor, so the rank-and-file orchestral musicians are expected to keep their pragmatic, sweaty, anxiety-laden lives out of view as much as possible.

With so much of their work kept hidden behind a facade of straight-laced, poker-faced elegance, audiences are often completely unaware of the extraordinary inner workings of professional orchestra "culture," and just how important those inner workings are to the making of the music.

Before I became a member of this exclusive club, I had the same grand preconceptions that most people have about professional orchestras, so the reality I encountered on the stage of Boston's Symphony Hall was a bit of a surprise, to say the least. But I always thought the reality of playing in a professional orchestra was far more interesting than the lofty fantasies produced by the press office. And so I am now going to violate the greatest taboo of the music business and tell you the real story of the often cynical, always stressful, sometimes hysterical, and occasionally magical world of the people who play notes for a living, whether it's for an opera, a Broadway show, or the Boston Pops—at least, as it was experienced by one young bass player. I admit these stories may put a dent in some of your fondest musical fantasies. But it is my sincere hope that, by seeing into this world (however strange it may seem to you at first) you will ultimately find yourself experiencing an even greater sense of connection to your favorite music.

Justin Locke
Boston, MA 2005

A Pops Tale

My bass teacher, a long time member of the Boston Symphony and the Boston Pops, swore that the following events actually took place, but he was such a loud liar we'll never know for sure.

This all supposedly happened back in the 1950's or 60's, in the days when the Boston Pops was conducted by Arthur Fiedler.

Before proceeding I should quickly mention that, while Arthur Fielder was beloved the world over by everyone else, several of the musicians in the Pops didn't like Arthur very much. There was one musician in particular, a Pops percussionist, who was always looking for ways to torment Arthur—without being so obvious about it that he would get fired.

Anyway, according to the story, the Boston Pops was playing a concert in a relatively small town somewhere in the middle of Massachusetts, with Arthur Fiedler conducting. They eventually came to the final piece on the program, which in this case happened to be Tchaikovsky's *1812 Overture*. The orchestra began to play the piece, just as they had played it hundreds of times before.

At first, everything was going along just fine. But then, about 20 bars into the piece, this percussionist (i.e., the one who liked to torment Arthur), well, I'm not sure how else to put it:

He threw up.

Mind you, he didn't throw up in the dressing room, and he didn't throw up off-stage.

He threw up . . . *on* the stage.

Obviously, this is not something you would want to have happen at any elegant event, much less an elegant event like a Pops concert, but orchestral musicians are human beings, and human beings, on occasion, do such things.

One would hope that this percussionist at least had the sense to do this behind a set of chimes, but wherever he did it, it was in full view of Arthur Fiedler, who immediately started to yell at this guy (quite audibly, by the way) to get off the stage. In response, the percussionist waved an apologetic hand motion to Arthur, and then he did indeed walk off stage.

At this juncture it is important to note that, in the world of professional orchestras, once you start playing the *1812 Overture* (or any other piece of music, for that matter), you *do not stop*—for *anything*. So the rest of the musicians kept right on playing, in spite of the gastronomic malfunction and labor/management dramatics that had just transpired.

With the percussionist now safely off stage, things returned somewhat to normal, or at least, as normal as they can be in such circumstances. But about 50 bars later, that very same percussionist came back out onto the stage . . . carrying a mop and a bucket. And he proceeded to clean up the mess he had made.

At this point, Arthur was turning three shades of indigo with veins popping out of his forehead. All the while the percussionist was making more of his little hand-waving signals, expressing his sincere apologies for having thrown up on stage in the first place—all this, in the middle of *1812*. And of course, while all the other musicians in the orchestra were experiencing internal hysterics, every single one of them did what professional orchestral musicians must always do in these situations: they kept right on playing (beautifully, I might add), pretending that nothing out of the ordinary was happening.

The percussionist got everything cleaned up, went off stage again, put everything away, and then, with a completely straight face, came back out to play his part in the big ending with all the chimes, cannons, tympani, cymbals, and snare drums. How could you fire him? He hadn't missed a single note.

I wasn't there, so I can't say that this story really happened, but given my experience with professional orchestral musicians, I have no reason to disbelieve it either.

Arthur

I am very proud to say that I once played for Arthur Fiedler. He was quite a character. Many books have been written about him, but none of them include the following, which is my favorite Arthur Fiedler story.

The Boston Pops plays concerts in Symphony Hall almost every night in May and June, and it sells lots of individual tickets to those concerts. It also does a brisk business selling large blocks of seats each night to various groups. Sometimes those group sales are so large, they take up every seat in Symphony Hall. To give you an example, a local university might buy out every seat in the hall for their 25th reunion. On another night a local corporation might buy every seat for that concert, and give them to their customers or employees. Some nights a convention might be in town and they would buy out every seat for their attendees. Whenever the audience was made up of one group like that, Arthur always tried to come up with a piece of music that was appropriate for them in some way.

One night, the American Guild of Organists was in town for their convention, and they had bought out the Hall. This meant that every single person in the audience that night was a professional organist. For this crowd, it was obvious that the "concerto" portion of the concert should be an organ concerto. To play the concerto, the guest soloist was E. Power Biggs. I suppose most people don't remember him any more, but in the mid-20th century, E. Power Biggs was the most famous organist in the USA. E. Power Biggs. What a fabulous name for an organ player.

"E." was getting on in years, but they managed to get him out onto the stage for what turned out to be his last public appearance with an orchestra. It was a fairly short little concerto though, so we needed to stretch that part of the concert with an encore. There aren't that many short pieces for organ and orchestra, so coming up with an encore took a little imagination.

What to do? Well, the members of the American Guild of Organists are all organists, of course. But by and large almost all of them are *church* organists, which means that almost all of them are also church choir directors. And we had 2,000 of them out there in the audience. So what did Fiedler do for an encore? He pulled out the *Hallelujah Chorus* from Handel's *Messiah*.

There was no chorus on the stage, but as I said, we had 2,000 choir directors out there in the audience. So Fiedler turned to the audience and, in his gruff voice, said: "We have an encore for you. We're going to play the *Hallelujah Chorus*. And we want you to be the chorus." He turned away from the audience, and then, in a typical bit of Fiedler showmanship, he turned to the audience once more and said, "You all know it—?"

This got a chuckle from the audience. Since they were all

church choir directors, every single one of them had conducted that piece hundreds of times, which meant that every one of them had the vocal parts memorized. So we started to play the *Hallelujah Chorus*—Arthur Fiedler, the Boston Pops, E. Power Biggs on the organ, and a *2,000*-voice choir, made up of professional choir directors. All this in Symphony Hall, one of the finest acoustic spaces in the world.

As is tradition whenever the *Hallelujah Chorus* is played, everyone in the audience stood up. What was *not* tradition was that they all started to sing. Oh boy, did they sing. This gigantic chorus included at least 500 slightly inebriated bass-baritone singers, plus 500 similarly intoxicated tenors, and when we got to the "King of kings" section . . . oh my God. They just tore the roof off the joint.

I played thousands of concerts in my professional bass playing career, and due to the Zen concentration that professional playing requires, I have few memories of specific moments in specific pieces on specific days. But that concert, I remember. I still get chills when I think about it.

What's even more remarkable about this concert was there was no rehearsal for it, and there was no audience to hear it.

*   *   *

When I played for Arthur Fiedler, I was seated by the stage entrance, so I always had to move out of his way when he walked on and off the stage. Most bass players have a cloth cover on their basses, hanging on the shoulders, to protect the bass's finish from belt buckle scratches. My cloth cover was made of red velvet. Every time Fiedler walked off the stage, he would pause next to me for just a moment and run his hand down this piece of velvet, as though he was petting a cat. He did that every single night. I have no idea why. It was just our little thing.

Climb Ev'ry Mountain

A lot of people presume that for an orchestra like the Boston Pops to sound as good as it does, it must rehearse constantly for several weeks before each concert. But the Pops actually rehearses very little. There are several reasons for this. First of all, no one really wants to rehearse, as rehearsals are dull and tedious and expensive. But the real reason the Pops doesn't rehearse all that much is because it simply isn't necessary.

It's easy to think of the players in a professional orchestra as being "very talented," but talent is just the beginning. Consider, for a moment, that every single one of the musicians up there on the stage has devoted their life to mastering their instrument, starting from age six or seven. Their technical prowess is pretty amazing—even when sight-reading a new piece, the notes are played at levels of near total perfection. Also, since everyone in the orchestra has played most of the pieces in the standard pop/symphonic repertoire dozens (if not hundreds) of times, they all already know "how it goes." And when you add to this their collective skill in terms of knowing how to play in any given style, both pop and classical, plus their ability to play so well together as an ensemble, well, when they do in fact rehearse, even if they are "sight-reading" a brand new piece, there is virtually no difference between how an orchestra like that sounds in rehearsal and how it sounds in a concert.

So, you might ask (and you would not be the first person to do so), what is the point of rehearsing at all? Well, there are always various little technical issues that need to be addressed, such as the choreography of moving guest artists on and off, where they will stand and sit, is their microphone working, and whatnot. Then there are always some pieces that require a clarification of the "road map," a slang professional musical term that refers to which repeats and/or cuts will be observed. (Obviously, if half the orchestra takes a cut and the other half doesn't, even at Pops there is a risk of a total musical meltdown.) And, if you're talking about a brand new arrangement, there is no knowing if the copyist[1] made any mistakes, so with new pieces it's always a good idea to "read it down," i.e., play it all the way through.

In Pops rehearsals, everyone speaks in a kind of musical shorthand. Everyone already knows the "famous places" that need clarification, and these are generally handled in very short order. At most rehearsals we would just run through any pieces we hadn't played for a while (as that was usually all we would need to do in order to see how the conductor wanted us to play a given piece), and everything would be fine.

However, some days weren't so fine. There was one rehearsal I played at Pops that was just so bizarre and strange

---

[1]Copyist: a person who takes the full score and writes out the parts, i.e., sheet music that has the notes for each individual instrument.

20

that it's hard to believe it actually happened, but it did.

At first, it was a rehearsal very much like every other. We covered most of the program, and eventually, it was time for the guest soloist to come out. The door behind the bass section opened up, and onto the stage walked a truly lovely young lady. She was in her early 20's, and she was very slim and extremely petite. She was introduced to the orchestra, and when we all looked at the music in our folders, there we saw . . . opera arias.

Opera arias? Right away we were all silently saying, "Hmmm, well, what is *this* . . .??" Classical music is a very tradition-heavy enterprise, and usually, when you see the sheet music for an opera aria in the folder, the next thing you should see is a woman of substantial girth waddling out on the stage. She should get an ice-cube-caught-in-her-throat look on her face, then she should begin to warble at about 95 decibels, and all is right in the world. This girl, well . . . she couldn't have weighed more than 80 pounds soaking wet. Single eyebrows were up everywhere, and puzzled glances were being surreptitiously exchanged all over the place. Not a word was said, but every look on every face was asking the same question: "Where is the fat lady?"

As it turned out, there was no fat lady. This little slip of a girl was all we had, and there was no time to fatten her up. So we ran through her two arias. This girl had a lovely sweet voice, but she didn't have a very big voice. No surprise there. Fortunately, the arias were by Donizetti, not Wagner, so we each played with one hair of our bows and just cut way back on our volume in general and, well, it was dicey but we got through it okay.

After we ran through these two arias, it was time to rehearse our guest soloist's encore. At a Pops concert, it's fairly typical for opera singers, after they've given you your minimum daily requirement of culture, to sing something from the pop/Broadway repertoire. Usually, their overly-trained voices are totally inappropriate for this lighter fare but no one, it seems, ever has the guts to tell them that, so . . . our guest had chosen *Climb Ev'ry Mountain* from *The Sound of Music.*

Our folders all contained the parts for the standard Pops vocal arrangement of *Climb Ev'ry Mountain*, which happened to be in the key of D major. So we played the intro, and our guest began to sing:

"Cliiimb ev'ry mountaaaain . . ."

At this point I need to mention a strange musical phenomenon that most civilians (i.e., non-musicians) don't know about: there are some people who have perfect pitch[2] and don't know it. They may not have a whole lot of musical talent otherwise, but once they learn a song in a certain key, well, that's it; they can't sing it in any other key. I guess you can tell what's coming. Our guest soloist had this brand of perfect pitch, and as the orchestra played the accompaniment in the key of D major, she began to sing . . . in G major. She was dead on, a consistent perfect fourth higher than the orchestra. And she did not stop.

"Foooooooord ev'ry streeeeeam . . ."

---

[2]Perfect pitch (also known as absolute pitch): the ability to recognize or sing any given musical pitch (e.g., A-flat) without reference to an instrument.

Everyone in the orchestra heard this, and of course we all immediately knew what was going on. Unfortunately, the guest conductor for this rehearsal (who shall remain nameless) did not. Now in his defense, conductors sometimes have a lot on their minds, and they are easily distracted. But this one didn't catch on . . . for a while. He knew *something* was wrong, but he couldn't quite figure out what. All the while this poor little girl was singing away, with the most wide-eyed look on her face—she knew something was wrong too but she couldn't figure it out either.

"Follllllllllow eeeeev'ry rainbooooooooow . . ."

Orchestras are used to having to hold in laughter every once in a while, but this was a special case. The problem was, two out of every three notes sounded sort of okay. It was the third one that got you. What were we to do? It's kind of rude to laugh at people when they're singing. It's even ruder to laugh at people when they are singing *Climb Ev'ry Mountain* in Symphony Hall.

Have you ever been in a high school study hall with a substitute teacher when something hysterical was going on? And you knew that, even though you weren't responsible, if you laughed out loud you'd be in the principal's office in no time? If you have, then you have some idea of what everyone in the orchestra was going through.

There was another problem though, one that was a little more serious. As I said, at a Pops rehearsal, totally correct playing of the notes is taken for granted, so there is no mechanism in the culture, nor is there any time in the schedule, for fixing wrong notes . . . at least, not this many of them all in a bunch. And time was quickly running out. When time runs short at a Pops rehearsal, the whole operation takes on an air of urgency, as there is a great desire to get through the piece at least once so as to check for any mistakes in the printed sheet music. So we kept on playing and playing. And our soloist kept on singing and singing.

"'Tillllllll . . . you fiiiiiind . . . your dreeeeeam . . .'"

Well, in spite of all the red faces, we managed to hold it in and keep on going. At least, we did until the trombones came in. Their notes were particularly loud and dissonant in relation to the singer, so the conductor decided that they were the culprits, and without stopping the music, he started to yell at them, accusing them of some kind of musical malfeasance.

This was too much. The assistant concertmaster couldn't take it anymore, so he just got up and ran off the stage. It all went downhill from there. The whole thing eventually just ground to a halt.

Even with a begrudgingly granted overtime period, and despite numerous starts, stops, and extensive conferences at the podium with the principal string players, we never did get through it at the rehearsal. This young lady simply would not sing this tune in any key other than G major, but the parts were in D major, and, well, eventually time just ran out. We all spent that afternoon wondering how the management was going to get around this little conundrum. When we came out to play it in the concert that night, sure enough, the only possible solution—an arrangement a fourth higher, in the key of G major—was in our folders. And it all went perfectly well.

*　　*　　*

The technical abilities of the players in major symphony orchestras are well illustrated by the following symphonic urban legend:

There was a young conductor who was going to conduct a major symphony orchestra for the first time. He wanted to impress the orchestra, so he hatched a clever little scheme: he would sneak into the library and write a wrong note in the second clarinet part. He would put this wrong note in a very dense and busy part of the music, where everyone was playing all at once. Then, in his first rehearsal, when the orchestra came to that place in the music, he would stop the orchestra and tell the second clarinetist about the mistake, thereby impressing everyone with his exceptional ear.

The night before his first rehearsal, he put his plan in motion. He crept into the library and, in a very dense part of the score, he found a B-flat in the second clarinet part and re-wrote it as a B-natural.

The next day, the rehearsal was going along, and at last the bar with the wrong note went by. Even though the conductor didn't really hear a wrong note, he stopped the orchestra and said, "Second clarinet, in bar 72, on the second 16th note, you played a B-*natural*. That should be a B-*flat*."

The conductor sat back and waited for the awe-filled oohs and ahhs of admiration to arise from this sea of professional musicians. But at this point the clarinetist casually replied:

"I *did* play a B flat. Some idiot copied the part wrong."

Symphonic Semantics

People often ask me, "What is the difference between the Boston Symphony and the Boston Pops?" Well, the short answer is, not very much, but since so many of the stories in this book are about my experiences in Boston's Symphony Hall, I think some brief definitions are in order.

Okay, to start, you have this very famous orchestra, made up of about 90 individual musicians, known as the Boston Symphony Orchestra (also known as the BSO). Their concert season ends each year on May 1st, more or less. The next day, that same group of musicians (with a few minor changes and substitutions) comes back to Symphony Hall. But now, instead of playing Mozart, they play Gershwin. And for about six weeks they call themselves the Boston Pops. Then, in the middle of June, they all pack up, head out to Tanglewood (their summer festival home in western Massachusetts), and call themselves the Boston Symphony again.

That's the quick answer, but from here on it gets complicated. As their name implies, the Boston Pops is very popular, and there is a huge demand for them to play concerts—all around the world, all year round. The trouble is, since the musicians who make up the Boston Pops are the same musicians who make up the Boston Symphony, during the symphony season they are too busy playing symphony concerts to also play all the Pops concerts that people are asking for.

To address this issue, some 30 years ago, the Boston Symphony management created a *second* Boston Pops Orchestra. Boston is something of a musical Mecca, with a very active community of very fine freelance musicians (many of whom came to Boston to study with members of the Boston Symphony), and about 90 of these freelance musicians are hired to make up this "other" Boston Pops Orchestra. This group plays the second half of the spring Pops season, they play the Fourth of July TV extravaganza, and they play many of the summer and Holiday Pops tours. For my first 10 years of playing in it, this second Pops orchestra was also called the Boston Pops. It was the same music, same conductors, same managers, same pay scale—just different players. And it is an excellent orchestra in its own right.

But at some point it was decided that there should be some difference in the names of these two Boston Pops orchestras. So now, if you see the name "Boston Pops," it means the orchestra is made up mostly of Boston Symphony musicians. And if (like on the Fourth of July) you see the name "Boston Pops Esplanade Orchestra," it means the orchestra is made up mostly of freelance players.

This differentiation is terribly important inside Symphony Hall, but when I try to explain it to people outside the culture, they often find it to be confusing. So for the sake of simplicity in telling my stories here, I don't use the term "Esplanade" very much, and my apologies to anyone who is offended by that approach. Just so you know, I was never an official member of the Boston Symphony, and most of the stories in this book are from my experiences in what is now generally referred to by folks in the biz as the "Esplanade Orchestra."

Baptism by Beethoven

There is a lot to be said for being in the audience for an orchestra concert. You get to sit back and relax and just listen, and that certainly has its merits. But in my opinion, that passive voyeuristic experience, however delightful it may be, pales in comparison to playing in the orchestra. For the musicians, the beauty and the sheer emotional power of the music is just the beginning. When you're up on the stage, at the moment the music starts, you suddenly find yourself in a state of intense, intimate, and total rhythmic connection with 90 other people. Playing in a great orchestra is the ultimate team sport. There is a tremendous sense of belonging, not just to a group, but to an elite group, and when you add the money, the fame, and the glamour, well, at times it is just delicious. Taken all together, playing in a major orchestra for the first time is an unforgettable experience. I will certainly never forget the first time I played in the Boston Pops.

It started casually enough. I had done some freelance playing in Boston one season while still in school. When summer came, I wasn't sure what else to do, so I went back home to Ohio. A few weeks later the phone rang, it was the Boston Pops, calling our house. (My mother was so excited.) So the personnel manager asked me if I wanted to play a week of

Pops in July. How in the world did they find my Ohio phone number? Well a paying gig is a paying gig, so I said "sure," without realizing that I was going to make less money for the week than it would take to transport myself and a bass to Boston and back. Oh well. You have to grab your breaks when they come.

Being something of a country bumpkin, I must confess that at the time I wasn't all that sure of just what the "Boston Pops" was. And, while I had some experience playing professionally in various local "gigs," I had not yet encountered the hard core, performing-night-after-night culture of a major symphony. So I walked into Symphony Hall for my first Pops rehearsal having no idea of what to expect. I certainly didn't expect what I got.

For most orchestral concerts, you generally have at least three or four rehearsals for a single program, but at Pops, this ratio of "rehearsals-to-programs" reverses—rather dramatically. My first day of Pops consisted of two rehearsals, in which we prepared the music, not for one program, not for two programs, but for *seven* programs we were to play that week. And what a week it was. In the space of only four hours and twenty minutes, we rehearsed:

Beethoven's 5th Symphony . . .
Beethoven's 7th Symphony . . .
Beethoven's 8th Symphony . . .
Sibelius' 2nd Symphony . . .
Mendelssohn's Italian Symphony . . . *and*
Tchaikovsky's 4th Symphony . . .

. . . plus all the "Pops" music we were going to play on the second half of each program, *and* the music for a family concert that included Prokofiev's *Peter and the Wolf.*

I use the word "rehearse" rather broadly here, as our rehearsing consisted of playing the first and last 16 bars or so of each movement, then quickly running through any sections in between that were known to be particularly nasty. That was it. You see, if you are playing in the Pops, it is simply assumed by all concerned that you already know all this music. But, being the new kid on the block, I didn't. I don't want to sound overly whiny here, but I have to tell you, the repertoire listed above is *hard* music, and in my young bass-playing career I had never played so many difficult notes in so many difficult pieces in such a short amount of time. I got through it, but I must confess that I walked out of there feeling rather dazed and confused.

Well, I had 24 hours to recover, and the following night I found myself out on the stage, all warmed up, and I was ready to play my very first Boston Pops concert. Or so I thought.

The conductor came out and, as is customary, the entire orchestra stood up for his entrance. But instead of everyone then proceeding to sit down to play Beethoven's 5th, everyone in the orchestra remained standing. I was not expecting this. Then, to my total surprise, the conductor pointed at the snare drum player, who proceeded to play a "roll," at which point everyone around me started to play *The Star Spangled Banner.*

I had no idea this was going to happen. It turns out the Pops always plays *The Star Spangled Banner* to begin its outdoor Esplanade concerts, but no one had bothered to tell me this. There was no sheet music for it on my stand, because every time the Pops plays *The Star Spangled Banner*, the entire orchestra improvises it, which is a nice way of saying they "fake it." And of course we had never rehearsed it.

So after all those years of lessons, practicing, and endless preparation, there I was, a 20-year-old farm boy from Ohio, all decked out in a recently purchased white tuxedo, up on the stage with the "big boys," eager to play the very first note of my very first Boston Pops concert, and not only was there no music on the stand, I didn't even know what key the piece was in. (Obviously, I know how to sing the melody of *The Star Spangled Banner*, but never once in the years I spent at the New England Conservatory, studying such important topics as the influence of the Flemish School and proper resolution of Neapolitan 6th chords, had anyone ever bothered to say to me, "Oh and by the way, if you want to be a professional bass player, you need to memorize the bass part to *The Star Spangled Banner*.")

Everyone in the audience was singing, and everyone on the stage was playing . . . except me. Did you ever have a nightmare where you were trying to do some simple task, like dialing a telephone, but you just couldn't do it, even though there was a dire need to do so? That's what this felt like. The whole experience was the stuff of nightmares, and yet it was actually happening.

Well, sink or swim. With no other option available, I just visually faked playing it. After the show, I went home in a much humbled state, and I stayed up late that night working out the chords and the harmony, and I memorized the bass part.

I still can't dial a phone in my dreams. But I tell you this: regardless of the circumstances—day, night, awake, asleep, or whatever—I assure you, I can play the bass part of *The Star Spangled Banner.*

*   *   *

Along with all the concerts the Boston Pops plays in Symphony Hall during the spring and in the holiday season, they also play lots of single concerts in neighboring cities. In Symphony Hall parlance, these concerts are called "run outs." This is because the orchestra will "run out" to Worcester or Providence to play the concert, and come back the same night.

A typical run out concert does not have a rehearsal beforehand. A rehearsal for a run out is generally unnecessary, because we would just play programs made up of pieces we had recently played dozens of times. But every once in a while, a single freelance player like myself would be hired to fill in for a regular BSO guy, and early in my Pops career I often found myself having to play a piece in concert that I had never played before.

They're certainly not going to schedule a whole rehearsal for just one piece for just one guy, so in this situation freelancers like myself had to just buck up and face the unknown. And facing the unknown in front of 20,000 adoring fans does tend to cause a certain amount of anxiety. So one night, early in my Pops career, when I had to deal with this for the first time, I openly expressed my angst. I said something like, "Gee whiz, I've never played this piece before."

A veteran member of the orchestra overheard this. In response, he put on his best feigned macho manner, and said:

"Real men don't rehearse."

Fourth of July

Way back in 1929, Arthur Fiedler started the tradition of a Fourth of July concert on Boston's Esplanade. (The Esplanade is a narrow park that runs along the shore of the Charles River.) Throughout its history, this outdoor patriotic musical evening had always attracted just a few thousand picnickers. So the freelance musicians (like me) who were hired to play the Fourth of July concert in 1976 didn't think too much about it. We figured it would be just like any other night on the Esplanade.

But in 1976, well, this was no ordinary Fourth of July. It was the Bicentennial. And there were going to be fireworks. And CBS was going to televise it. So the Esplanade suddenly became *the* place to go. Instead of hanging out at the beach or staying home for a barbecue, throughout the day, more and more people made their way to the Hatch Shell[3]. At first they came in hundreds, then they came in thousands, and then they came in tens of thousands. Eventually, instead of the usual crowd of maybe five thousand people, five *hundred* thousand

---

[3]The Hatch Shell, an acoustical shell located on Boston's Esplanade, was built in 1928 (rebuilt in 1941) as a memorial to Edwin M. Hatch. It was a gift to the city from Edwin's sister, Maria.

people just happened to show up. At the time, it was the largest audience that had ever come to a concert of classical music.

The police were totally unprepared for this onslaught. Normally, for a crowd of this magnitude there would be traffic cones and blue sawhorses everywhere, but there were none. Crowd control was virtually non-existent. And even if there was . . . where could they put all these people? The park was only so big, with a road on one side and the river on the other. People just jammed themselves in anywhere they could.

At 7:00 p.m., an hour before the concert was supposed to start, my colleagues and I boarded three buses that would take us to the Hatch Shell on the Esplanade. Boston has many one-way streets and low bridges, so the buses always had to take a circuitous route. The trip was made a little easier this time by an escort of motorcycle police. With sirens wailing, they darted around us like a pack of sheepdogs as we gleefully ran through red lights all over town. But when we got to the Esplanade, even a police escort could not get us to our usual unloading spot. There were so many people gathered around the Hatch Shell that the road next to it had become completely jammed. There was simply no way any vehicle could get through that solid mass of humanity.

What to do? The musicians had to get in there somehow. Fortunately, the road next to the Esplanade had a concrete traffic divider running down the middle that was topped by a chain link fence, and that kept most of the crowd from spilling over into the far side of the roadway. So the buses used that side of the road instead, pulling up as close as they could to the Hatch Shell.

So far, so good. But now there was still that concrete traffic divider, the chain link fence, and a solid mass of people between us and our destination.

I had an added complication: instead of having my bass shipped down to the Hatch Shell in a trunk like everyone else, for some reason I had mine with me. As I got off the bus lugging my bass, I followed the line of my formally attired colleagues to a spot where two burly policemen lifted me up to the top of the concrete traffic divider. Then I had to slip through a hole that had been hastily cut in the chain link fence, taking care not to rip my tuxedo on the jagged edges. Once I was through, two more policemen lowered me down on the other side. Then they passed my bass through the narrow jailbreak opening in the fence and handed it down to me.

Now that the first obstacle had been overcome, we all had to somehow make our way through the crowd that filled every inch of space between the hole in the fence and the stage door of the Hatch Shell. To do this called for yet another bit of hasty pragmatism: two lines of backward-leaning police officers had carved out a narrow aisle, just big enough for the black-and-white caravan of musicians to make their way to the shell. So in we went, in narrow single file, surrounded by adoring fans.

When you enter the stage door of the Hatch Shell, you have two choices: you can go right, into the locker area, or you can take a left and go up the stairs to the stage. While everyone else went to the right, I decided it would be easier to unpack my bass right where I was going to play it, so I went left, up the steps, to the stage.

When I emerged from the narrow confines of the staircase, my jaw dropped. There, out in the park in front of the Hatch Shell, were people—people, people, everywhere, as far as the eye could see. 500,000 of them. They were on every sidewalk, every blade of grass, every rock, and every tree branch. The Charles River was a solid mass of yachts and rowboats, filled with still more people.

Once I recovered from the initial shock of viewing this astonishing spectacle, it slowly dawned on me that I was the very first musician to arrive on the stage, which also meant that, at that moment, I was the *only* musician on the stage. I could hear a low murmur slowly building in the crowd, as these many thousands upon thousands of people were all looking at, talking about, and pointing at . . . *me.*

Well, I couldn't very well ignore them, so, not being sure of what else to do, I raised my hand to wave "hello."

This massive audience had spent much of the day in the hot sun, waiting and waiting for the concert to begin, so when they saw this first small spark of greeting from one of the real live Pops musicians, their collective anticipation exploded into a massive rolling thunder of cheers and applause. It made its way up through the crowd, beyond the trees, up the river, and all the way to the next town over. I was the lone recipient of this massive ovation.

A career in music has many downsides—the practicing, the stress, the hours, the politics . . . but at that one shining moment, it all seemed very worthwhile.

A Bass Viol Thing to Do

Like any culture, a big part of belonging to orchestral culture is knowing its many traditions. Some orchestral traditions are common to all orchestras. But some traditions are specific to individual orchestras.

The Boston Pops has many little unusual traditions, most of which are only done in certain pieces of music. For example, in Leroy Anderson's *Fiddle Faddle*, there is a part of the piece, about halfway through, where the Pops brass section always stands up and sings their part instead of playing it. Since the brass players always, *always*, did this whenever we played the piece, I just assumed it was written that way in the score, but one day I looked at a score and it was nowhere to be found. Who knows how it started, I suppose one day some bored trumpet player started singing along and it just snowballed. Sometimes, along with the singing, they stand up and do a little Supremes-style arm choreography too. Many other orchestras play this piece, but I have never seen anyone but the Pops brass do the singing.

In another Leroy Anderson piece, *Bugler's Holiday*, there is a spot about halfway through, where there is a silent third beat of a bar, right after which the entire orchestra plays a big bang on the fourth beat. To play together on that fourth "off" beat, the orchestra really needs to *feel* that silent third beat, and I suspect that once upon a time somebody grunted—either as a joke or unconsciously—on that third beat, and it just grew from there, to the point where it's now a Pops tradition for the *entire orchestra* to go "UHHH!!!" on that silent third beat. It's pretty amusing to hear 90 people doing that all at once in a concert in Symphony Hall. But that's only done in live shows. You'll never hear it on a recording or on TV. Whenever we were going to play that piece on TV, the personnel managers would come around and say, "No grunting tonight . . . no grunts . . ." And we would all moan like disappointed school children in response. But in a regular live show, it's always there . . . louder or softer, depending on how we think the conductor will handle it.

Most pieces of orchestral music have little sections where various members of the orchestra are required to play a little solo. Some of these solo sections are known to be very difficult. So, in rehearsal, when someone in an orchestra executes a difficult solo well and deserves applause, the orchestra does not applaud in the usual way, since everyone's hands are full. Instead, the orchestra will shuffle its feet. But at Pops, this sort of peer adulation has an amusing little dark side. There is one little spot in *Richard Rogers Waltzes* where the first horn has a solo. It's a short, simple, schmaltzy little broken chord—not even the main melody, easy to play, no big deal really . . . but every time the first horn plays this simple solo in rehearsal, the entire orchestra will shuffle its feet in wild sarcastic foot-applause. Sometimes we would do this in concerts too. Don't ask me why. It's just tradition.

Another time-honored Pops tradition: in many Holiday Pops concerts, the orchestra will play the famous Pops arrangement of *White Christmas*. This excellent arrangement includes a very sweet, sentimental violin solo. As the concertmaster plays this solo, other members of the orchestra will sometimes throw quarters on the floor at the soloist's feet, implying that the concertmaster is an itinerant street musician playing for spare change. Symphony Hall being the acoustic marvel that it is, when those quarters hit the floor you can hear them all the way up to the back of the second balcony. The audience always thinks this is just a bizarre accident, but it isn't. It's musician humor, and it's a Pops tradition.

The grandest Pops tradition though (at least in my opinion), has to do with bass section choreography.[4] If all seven players do the same motion with such large instruments in time with the music, the audience just loves it. So over the years, various "moves" have been choreographed to specific spots in specific pieces. For example, in *St. Louis Blues March*, there is a spot where we would do a "wave." On each of seven successive beats, one player after another would lift their bass, making a "wave" down the row, and then we would lift them up all together on the eighth beat.

There were other little things we would do, but the most popular bass section choreography was doing a big section

---

[4]Pops Bass section choreography was largely created (I think) by a guy name John Barwicki, who played in the BSO for years and years. What a character. Just to give you an idea: when the BSO goes to Tanglewood for the summer, the players are given a housing allowance to cover the expense of living there. Most of them use that money to pay for a cabin by a lake, but Barwicki would just pitch a tent on BSO property by the Stockbridge Bowl. Every summer he lived in the wild for eight weeks, and pocketed the housing allowance. At age 80 he used to buzz around town on a motorcycle. He had a lot of style.

"spin." Seven double basses, twirling around, starting and stopping all together, is a pretty impressive sight.

As I mentioned, there are two Boston Pops orchestras, and I'm not exactly sure when or how this happened, but it just gradually came about that I became the de facto choreographer for the Esplanade Pops bass section. When we all came out for the final third of a concert, all the other bass players would look at me and ask, "Are we spinning tonight?" And I would tell them the plan for the evening.

Spinning a bass may sound simple, but doing it right is not so simple. Before the spin, we all had to move our music stands around a little and set ourselves up with enough room to avoid any nasty 78 RPM collisions. To punch up the effect, just before the spin we would do a little waving of our bows, and maybe even a little shouting in order to get the crowd's attention. And two beats before the spin I would usually call out a "ready . . . AND!" to get everyone started all together, which is the key to the visual effectiveness of it.

Also, you can't just spin a bass any old time. Part of the "art" of it is to find a spot in the music where it's appropriate. There are plenty of Pops arrangements with a good "spin spot," enough that we could usually do one every night. The crowd always loved it, and some guest conductors would actually program certain pieces specifically because they contained good bass section spin spots.

When John Williams came on board as the Music Director, well, he was a little ambivalent about the bass spinning. It was a Pops tradition, so he tolerated it, although he was never really excited about it. Despite the enormous emotional power of the music he writes, John Williams is, in every day life, an exceptionally quiet guy. So all this obstreperous unrehearsed shouting and spinning in public was not really his thing. But, like I said, he put up with it.

At least, he did until we went on our first tour to Japan.

When we got to Japan, we looked at the programs, and it became apparent that *none* of the pieces in which we usually did a bass spin were on either of the two programs we were playing on that tour. The library was 10,000 miles away. So *that* was *that*. "Okay, Maestro," I said to myself. "I get the hint. We can fool around on our own turf but when we're playing in Japan we need to tone it down." The message was subtle but very clear. I mean, you have to work pretty hard to come up with two entire programs' worth of Pops music and not have any bass spin spots in them. And he had.

So the tour was going along, with no bass spins. I didn't think very much about it, as I had grieved the loss and moved on. But on the third night, Kim Smedvig, the press office director, came up to me backstage, all in a dither. "Justin!" she said. "The basses aren't spinning!!"

"Uh huh," I said. "And your point is . . .?"

"Well," she said, "the promoters are VERY UPSET!"

It turned out that one of the reasons the promoters thought we would be so well received in Japan was because of all this highly-unusual-for-an-orchestra-to-be-doing clowning around they saw us doing in Boston, i.e., bass spinning. (Not that anyone had ever mentioned this to us bass players.) So I tried, as best I could, to explain to her that there was no music for us to spin *to*, but at this point communication between us sort of broke down. She just kept saying, "The promoters are very upset, you have to spin the basses, the promoters are very upset, you have to spin the basses . . ." And then she just walked away.

Okay, obviously the conductor wanted one thing and the press office and the promoters wanted the opposite, and there I was, just the lowly nameless fifth chair bass player with no contract to speak of who is damned if he does and damned if he doesn't. Why was it my job to worry about this?

Well, it wasn't like anyone had specifically told me *not* to spin the basses, so I pulled out the bass folder and, after a fair amount of digging, lo and behold, I found a potential spin spot that no one had ever noticed before, in *76 Trombones*.

I was reasonably sure this would be a good spin spot, but there was no knowing for sure until we actually did it. So, just to help things along the first time out, I enlisted the aid of the percussion section, asking them to add a few extra notes.

That night, the moment came. Big percussion bang. We all spun the basses. Perfect unison start and stop. The crowd went nuts. The promoters and the press office were happy again. I could see them all standing in the wings, happily bowing and smiling to each other.

The wild applause for our bass spin gradually died down. John Williams, being no dummy, knew exactly who had instigated all this, and for the remaining 16 bars of the piece he looked right at me, nodding his head like a good loser, with a *you-son-of-a-(etc.), you-got-me-this-time* smile on his face.

*　　*　　*

One night, the Pops was playing for a convention in a hotel ballroom in Boston. John Barwicki, the original bass section choreographer, was playing, and in the middle of an encore he had the section do a bass spin. Unfortunately, in his zeal to spin his own bass, John had forgotten the number one rule of bass spinning, which is . . . check your clearances. He gave his bass a big shove, but instead of twirling, it went right into a cellist's chair, making a most terrifying crunching noise. His bass—a very old instrument that had not been cleaned out in living memory—split all the way up one side, and everyone saw a little mushroom cloud of dust rising out of the bass section.

Pecking Orders

Unlike painters, writers, or other "artists" who tend to work alone and at their own pace, orchestras are rather large conglomerates of artists who must work very closely together, in both space and time. (Imagine for a moment if, at your job, you had to constantly share your desk with another person, and on top of that you had to make every single keystroke at your computer in exact rhythmic unison, not just with them, but also with 90 of your co-workers. If you can imagine that, then you have some idea of what it's like to work in a professional orchestra.) Melding the talents and energies of 90 narcissistic artistic individuals into one cohesive unit that moves in exact rhythmic sync at all times requires the imposition of a considerable amount of structure and discipline. In spite of all the "art" that is going on, orchestras are actually highly regimented organizations whose operation resembles, more than anything else, the military. It is common for outsiders to think that this extreme level of organization is being imposed on a bunch of rowdy ne'er-do-wells by the conductor, but the conductor actually has very little to do with it. This kind of intense structure is an inherent element of professional orchestras.

While every orchestral musician knows this system all too

well, I have never seen it written down anywhere. So for all you outsiders, I will attempt to codify it.

Every orchestra follows a strict system of cascading authority. Starting at the top, well, I suppose everyone knows that the conductor, at least in theory, is at the top of the chain of command. (The next time you go to a concert, you will notice that, like the military, the orchestra "comes to attention" when the conductor enters.)

After the conductor, the person with the next highest level of authority in an orchestra is the principal first violinist, who is also known as the concertmaster. The concertmaster, who is seated just to the left of the conductor, is sort of like the top sergeant. When the conductor enters, or when he asks the orchestra to stand for a bow, everyone in the orchestra watches the concertmaster. When the concertmaster stands, we stand. When he sits, we sit. When the applause is dying down at the end of a concert, we look at the concertmaster. When he walks off, we walk off. The concertmaster's job also includes, and I kid you not, taking over as conductor in case the conductor drops dead in the middle of the show. Like I said, it's very much a military operation, and casualties happen. One must plan for such contingencies. Another immutable custom of orchestral pecking orders: if the concertmaster's violin breaks in the middle of a concert, it is the solemn duty of the second chair violinist to hand their violin over to the concertmaster to play until the broken violin can be fixed. This is the case even when you're talking about the second chair violinist having to hand over (to someone that they may not like all that much) a violin that cost well over $100,000 and hasn't been paid for yet.[5]

After the concertmaster, the next level of authority is assigned to the section leaders, who are also known as the "first chair" or "principal" players. Each section of instruments (the trumpet section, the cello section, etc.) has a section leader. (The concertmaster is the section leader of the first violin section. There is also a section leader of the second violin section. I never said this was easy.)

When you're in the middle of performing a piece of music, there is no time for committee meetings. So if there is ever any difference of opinion about how something should be played (and when is there not?), the section players must immediately and unquestioningly defer to their section leader's opinion. In the string sections, the section leaders also determine the section's "bowings"—in each string section, everyone's bow has to change direction in precise lock step with the principal player throughout the entire concert. There are no exceptions. Also, section string players are not allowed to speak to the conductor. If a section player has a question, they must direct that question first to their section leader, and if the section leader can't answer it themselves, and if they deem it necessary, they will pass it on to the conductor. (Winds, brass, and percussion players are

---

[5]In the case of a broken string, the second chair player will usually just fix it on the spot and then swap it back. For a larger repair, the second chair player may leave the stage at an appropriate moment. When this happens, or in the case of anyone in a string section not showing up, or passing out (or worse), different orchestras have different "move up" policies (e.g., everyone moves up a chair, or the last chair player moves up to fill in the empty seat). Again, like the military, it's important to close up those ranks.

48

a little different. They can sometimes speak directly to the conductor, since they are all playing different parts—but section string players? Never, never, never.)

The ranking doesn't stop there. After the section leaders, each player in a section is assigned a specific number or rank, known as their "seating assignment." For example, you might be the third trombone or the fourth trumpet. For string players, the numbering system is a little more dehumanized. Your chair is given a number, and you just sit in it. For example, I was the "fifth chair bass."

This numbering of players has all sorts of practical applications—for example, if the music in your instrument's part "divisi's" (i.e., divides) into two parts, everyone automatically knows, by their number, which part they are supposed to play (odds play the top, evens play the bottom). And, if you are sharing a music stand, the lower ranked person always turns pages for the higher ranked person.

But along with these practical applications, these seating assignments within sections also carry with them a troubling sort of symbolism, because seating assignments imply gradations of quality. In theory, in each section, the first chair player is better than the second chair, the second chair player is better than the third, and so on.

As a result, your seating assignment takes on enormous emotional importance: it represents the management's official assessment of your personal ability as a musician. Of course, like most workplaces, politics and seniority have as much to do with where you're seated as anything else. But the musicians are rarely objective or open-minded about it. Your playing is a very personal thing, and any comments or judgments about it (and a seating assignment is a very powerful public statement on that topic) are a very big deal. Higher seating offers a delicious sense of artistic superiority to those seated beneath you. ("I may not be the best, but at least I'm better than *you*.") Higher seating also has a very practical benefit: it often has a lot to do with who gets hired first for extra work. And so you can well imagine, when you combine the social status with the money (and when you add in the rivalries that have been going on between some musicians since grade school), well, it is often an emotionally charged issue, and people take it very seriously. "Who sits ahead of whom" is a never-ending topic of discussion amongst musicians, as it brings up the eternal questions of who is better than whom, who has studied with whom, who is sucking up more than whom, and who is sleeping with whom.

The following little story will give you an idea of just how important seating assignments are in orchestral culture: The first time I was called to "sub" in the Boston Symphony, I was to fill in for a guy who had been the second chair bass player in the BSO for many years. Why wasn't he there? Well, another bass player, the one who had been the *first* chair bass player for decades, had recently retired, and this second chair guy was hoping to move up a notch. But when the audition for the first chair bass position was held, things went awry. Someone else, from another orchestra, got the job.

After years and years of being number two, here was this guy's once-in-a-lifetime chance for a promotion, and he didn't get it. So he went home, thought it over for a while, and shot himself in the head.

Flying on Instruments

I once encountered a situation in a concert that was so bizarre that even the time-honored rules of seating protocol didn't cover it.

Most standard Pops concerts include a concerto. A concerto is a piece that has a soloist who is accompanied by the orchestra. (A concerto is always for an instrument, not a singer, and is referred to by the solo instrument—e.g., a piano concerto, a trumpet concerto, etc.) Most concerto soloists at Pops were either pianists or violinists, but not always. There are concertos written for just about any instrument you care to name.

Concertos always carry with them an added level of difficulty, because while the orchestra always has to follow the conductor, in a concerto, the conductor has to follow the soloist, and with so many cooks stirring the tempo, the possibility of a major musical train wreck is never very far away.

On this particular evening we were playing the Ginastera *Harp Concerto.* I have nothing against Ginastera per se, but at Pops it was always an adventure when we played a piece that was not in the standard warhorse chestnut repertoire, because we generally only had one rehearsal, and that rehearsal wasn't much more than a run-through, at that.

The Ginastera *Harp Concerto* is a "contemporary" piece, and it is somewhat *atonal*, a fancy musical term that means that if you play a wrong note, there's a good chance no one will notice. This was a good thing, because most of us didn't know this piece, and it was pretty hard to play.

Since harps don't play very loud, there was a reduced number of string players for this concerto: only four basses instead of the usual seven.

The bass section at Pops is usually set up in two rows. The first two bass players usually have their own row, and the rest of the section sits in another row behind them. This meant that for this piece, my stand partner (a guy I'll call Ralph) and I, who were the third and fourth chair basses, were seated directly behind the first two bass players. We could see them of course, but they would have to turn around to see us.

On the second page of the bass part, there was a four-bar bass solo that was to be played only by the first and second chair bass players. So, since Ralph and I were the third and fourth chair players, during this solo section all we had to do was sit back and watch.

Well, the piece started and things were going along at a pretty good clip. And since (outside of one rehearsal) no one in the orchestra had ever played or even heard this piece before, the whole experience was a bit of a stress test.

Things were going well enough—that is, until I turned the

first page. At that moment Ralph and I came to the sudden realization that we were not playing anything remotely like what the first two bass players were playing. Ralph gave me a look that said, "You idiot, you must have turned two pages" . . . but lo and behold, a quick check and we realized that no, I had not turned two pages—it was the *first and second chair basses* who had turned two pages.

And they had not noticed.

As strange as this may seem, instead of playing the notes on page *two*, these guys were now playing the notes on page *four*. (Like I said, the piece was "modern" and atonal enough that it wasn't immediately obvious to them that the notes they were playing were really and truly "wrong"—so they played and played . . . .)

Ralph and I had both been at Pops for a few years longer than these two guys, but, for reasons never fully explained, these two rookies, who had both just graduated from a local music school, had been seated ahead of us that summer—quite a slap in the face in orchestral culture. Naturally, there is a certain amount of resentment when this sort of unexpected anomaly in the pecking order occurs, so neither Ralph nor I were all that motivated to rescue these guys.

The trouble was, the four bar solo section for the first two basses (on page *two*) was coming up, so Ralph and I were faced with a unique artistic dilemma that had to be resolved in about eight bars. One thing I forgot to mention about orchestral hierarchies: in orchestral culture, the one thing that supersedes the authority of everyone on the stage, including the conductor, is the composer. Well, actually, the composer himself, who cares, but the *notes* . . . the notes on the page are viewed with no less reverence than the words of a prophet of a religious order. As professional orchestral players, every fiber of our being was devoted to playing the notes laid down by the composer. But obviously, under the current circumstances, this was not going to happen. So—should we step in and play the part?? Hmmm . . . well, if our new young stars on the first stand were somehow physically incapacitated, of course we would. And if their basses had fallen apart or broken a string, of course we would. But they, and their instruments, were perfectly functional. And the very idea of playing someone else's solo, unannounced, just because we didn't think they were going to do it right . . . well, gee whiz, now you're talking about a major breach of 500 years' worth of orchestral protocol. Plus, the notes were kind of hard, and since we hadn't planned on playing them, we hadn't practiced them.

There was yet one more difficulty facing us: we were right on the edge of the stage, so the front row of the audience was only about 12 feet away. This meant we had to resolve the situation using only non-verbal communication. For the next 15 seconds, in a language known only to orchestral stand partners, we had an extensive conference, using eyebrow raising, head tipping, and shoulder shrugging. Alas, we failed to reach a consensus. With only one bar left to ponder the situation, discretion and cowardice took over and, despite terrible feelings of professional shame and artistic guilt, we just remained stock still and watched the correct notes go by—unplayed—while the rookies on the first stand were, by this time, playing something on page five.

As the piece continued on, Ralph and I had our hands full just playing the correct notes, but even so we could not help but be fascinated by the sight of these two guys in front of us playing all these random pitches.

These two youngsters were so totally focused, and so totally sincere, and the notes were so totally wrong, that pretty soon Ralph and I found ourselves fighting off a severe case of the giggles. I should point out that in Pops culture, playing a few wrong notes, while highly frowned upon, is a forgivable offense, but allowing the audience to see you laughing hysterically in the middle of a harp concerto . . . is not.

The current situation, if left unchecked, was certain to bring us perilously close to losing all control and maybe even getting fired. So, with a quick poke in our colleagues' backs with a bow (actually, it took a few pokes), a little reverse page-turn hand signaling, and a loudly whispered "Bar 194!", we all got back on track . . . and no one was ever the wiser.

What Is a Lunch?

Every three years or so, lawyers hired by the managements of major symphony orchestras sit down with lawyers hired by the local musician's unions to hammer out details of the musicians' contract. These contracts (known as the "Trade Agreement") delineate everything—and I do mean everything—in astonishing detail, such as the length of rehearsals and concerts, the number of days off each week, what constitutes overtime, and so on and so forth.

Of course, once you get lawyers involved, no detail is too small to be examined at great length. The excruciating minutiae that were hashed out in these discussions often felt like a script for a Seinfeld episode. They were right out of a show about nothing.

Before I go on, I need to quickly explain something: whenever the Pops goes on tour, the pay scale calls for each player to get something like $65 a day in "per diem" money to pay for meals. This figure is based on the idea that eating in a hotel usually costs $15 for breakfast, $20 for lunch, and $30 for dinner. This may seem like a lot to some people, but very often the Pops management would book us into hotels that were nowhere near anything even remotely resembling civilization, so we *had* to eat at the hotel's restaurant, and that really did cost $65 dollars a day. But to be honest, in practice, whenever possible we would pocket most of the wonderfully tax-free per diem money and run across the street and eat at Denny's for three bucks.

Per diem money was always wonderful to get, but there was one exception to the per diem rule: if the symphony management *provided* a catered breakfast, lunch, or dinner while we were on a tour, they didn't have to pay the orchestra any per diem for that meal. Seems simple, but . . . not so simple. One summer, the biggest point of contention in the Symphony/Pops' labor-management contract negotiations was not about Mahler or Bruckner or Mozart. It was all about the terribly difficult question of . . . "What is a lunch?"

Specifically, if you are flying on an airplane from 10 a.m. to 2 p.m. and you get served lunch on the plane, is this airplane meal . . . a meal? Or does the symphony management have to give you your $20 of per diem for lunch?

I cannot begin to tell you the extraordinary degree to which this question was analyzed from every conceivable angle. What makes a meal a meal? Is it when you eat it? Is it the number of calories consumed within a given time frame? Is it something to do with the quality or quantity of the food? Does it have anything to do with the aesthetic experience of eating off a plastic vs. a ceramic plate? Is it the limited choice of meat or fish? Being an amateur philosopher, I began to ponder this imponderable myself, and I took great pleasure in sharing my questioning with the management. I kept coming up with possible exceptions to the per diem rules. Whenever I walked past a manager at a catered meal, I would ask a question like, "I didn't finish my dessert. Can

I have $5 of my per diem back?"

This sort of thing went on all summer, as I posed more and more variations on this question to a management team that was already sick of hearing the arguments about this from all the other players.

One night we were playing a concert in New York. The orchestra had been fed a catered meal at the venue (so, no dinner per diem money). We were going to fly back to Boston that night, right after the show. This posed yet another possible scenario that I felt should be included in the contract negotiations. I posed this question to a manager that night, and even she had to crack a smile. I asked:

"On the way back to Boston, if I throw up on the plane, do I get my per diem for the dinner?"

Til Retirement Do You Part

One element of professional orchestra playing that no one ever warns you about is the "arranged marriage" that occurs when you are assigned a stand partner. For string players in major orchestras, it is not uncommon to have the same stand partner for 10, or maybe even 20 years (or more). There is never any choice of where you sit or who sits next to you; this is all pre-determined by whoever hires you.

Like any marriage, a stand partner can be a wonderful experience, or it can be hell on earth. I have heard stories of people in professional orchestras who have shared the same stand for decades at a time and no one can remember the last time they spoke to each other.

When you spend that many years on the same stand with someone, well, if you *are* on speaking terms, you get to know them really well. There are so many times when the rehearsal is interrupted, and there's nowhere to go, and the only person you have to talk to is your stand partner. So you hear all about whatever happened today with mom and the cousins and the car. Anything to pass the time. Also, in string sections, you are always playing the exact same part as your stand partner, so you're both constantly getting to know each other's styles so you can blend with them. After a while you get to be like an old married couple that always wins at bridge, although no one can ever catch them cheating. You know exactly what your stand partner is thinking just by little changes in body language.

Sharing a stand with someone, and just playing in an orchestra in general, is a somewhat claustrophobic experience. It's rare that the stage in an older concert hall has enough room for a full symphony orchestra to spread out comfortably, and even if it does, you still have to sit close enough to your stand partner so that you can both see the sheet music on the music stand you are sharing. Then the players behind you, in front of you, or next to you always want you to move this way or that way so they can have more room or see the conductor. You can never get yourself settled in from one concert to the next, because in between rehearsals and performances the stage is constantly being cleared off and re-set for one reason or another, and afterwards the stagehands just rough the chairs and stands back in. Also, very often during the intermission a piano will be rolled right through the bass section. With each disruption, the whole process of fine-tuning your location and negotiating for personal space starts all over again. There are times when you feel like a lab rat in some sort of experiment, where they have put too many of you into a cage to see how you cope with the stress. (Of course, the space issues on a stage are nothing compared to the experience of playing in the pit of a small theater, where everyone is crammed in there like a subway in Rome.)

Along with all the niggling little territorial issues involved in sharing a music stand, another ongoing issue in stand partner land is page turns. Whatever stand you're on, orchestral protocol strictly dictates that whoever is lower-ranked turns the pages, while the higher-ranked player plays through the page turn. Page turning is a big part of your musical communication with your stand partner, and it's an art in itself.

Depending on the complexity of the music, your average musician can memorize maybe three bars ahead of where he is playing right now. For the person turning pages, here is the trick: you have to turn the page at the exact moment when your stand partner has memorized to the end of the page, and then get it over in time for your stand partner to see, mentally digest, and play the notes on the following page, without any notes being dropped in the process. This is not easy. If you are the page turner, you must be quick; you must be precise in your timing; you must not turn two pages; you must not drop your bow; and you must not make a big "thwack" noise in the middle of Barber's *Adagio for Strings*.

I always prided myself on my page turning ability. But sometimes I would be the higher-ranked, odd-numbered player on my stand, and I would have to endure someone else turning my pages for me, as there was no getting around the rule. Some stand partners were okay. But there were others who would put their thumb over the last two bars of music, and, long after the time to turn the page had come and gone, they would be feverishly staring at me with a "Now? Now??" look in their eyes.

One of my favorite stand partners was Ralph, the guy I mentioned in the last chapter. (This is a pseudonym, as he is still in the music business.) We played something like 400 Nutcrackers together, and suffering through so much with someone, note for note, is a bond like no other.

Ralph was famous for his pithy little comments. When I showed up for my very first professional job, Ralph was standing next to me; I had heard of him, but it was the first time we had ever met. I was a little nervous since I was so new, and I was only 19 years old. So he sized me up, then he looked at me very matter-of-factly and said, "Can I give you some advice?"

"Sure, sure," I said, waiting for some grand piece of musical wisdom to be bestowed upon me.

He said, and I quote:

"Don't be a hero."

What he meant was, "If you're not sure if you're supposed to play . . . don't." It was some of the best advice I have ever been given.

It's a Dirty Job but Someone Has to Do It

Within the culture of symphony orchestras, there are subcultures for each instrument. This is because players of a given instrument all have certain things in common that they do not have in common with other players. For example, in each section, you share the same technical challenges specific to your instrument, you occasionally discuss the current market for new instruments, you often have the same teachers, and so on. (There's nothing worse than getting on a plane and finding yourself stuck amongst a bunch of oboe and bassoon players, discussing reed suppliers for two hours.)

I am not really qualified to discuss the inner workings of the cultures of other instruments, but for what it's worth, here is a brief introduction to "bass culture."

Bass players differ from all the other members of every orchestra in one very basic way: no bass player, at least to my knowledge, ever chose to be a bass player. You will never see a kid in front of a music store window, pointing at a string bass, crying out, "Mommy, I wanna play *that*." While all the other members of the orchestra had loving parents who bought them their first shiny flute or took them to harp lessons every Saturday at the conservatory, bass players are, for the most part, the reluctant "draftees" of the orchestra. We all just got talked into it for one reason or another. The typical story told by a bass player is, "I showed up late the day they had band sign-ups, there were no other instruments left, I was big for my age, and no one else wanted to do it."[6]

My own story is very similar—while in high school, my older sister had been pressed into service as a bass player, and, since she was the only bass player in three counties, she instantly found herself bopping all over northwestern Ohio, playing in this band and that orchestra. To a 12-year old kid marooned on a dirt farm this sounded like fun, and a good way to get out of the house. So, having nothing else to do one summer's day, I slid my sister's bass out from under the piano, opened up a "how-to" book to page one, and started to saw away. It's not that I really wanted to be a bass player. I was just bored, and looking for something to do.

Well, once you play that first bass note, it's sort of like opening a bag of potato chips. Perhaps you had no conscious expectation of eating more than one, but before you know it the situation has gotten out of hand. This is because, at the student level, playing the string bass is not about talent or skill. It's all about supply and demand.

It's very much different for other instruments. For example, if you're one of those hundreds of flute players out there, and you're a real superstar, you *might* get accepted to this school or that program, and *maybe* get a small scholarship

---

[6]My stand partner, Ralph, had the best of these stories I think. When anyone asked him how he ended up playing the bass, he would always give the same answer. He would say, "I don't know—I just woke up one morning and it was in bed with me."

(depending on how many other superstar flute players there are this season). But since bass players are so rare, you don't have to be terribly good, or even all that motivated, to be wonderfully successful at it. Once I had mastered most of the C major scale, it didn't matter where I applied; whether it was a summer camp, a festival in Switzerland, or a national youth orchestra in Carnegie Hall, I was immediately accepted—if not actively recruited. I never once got turned down for anything. I really wasn't very good, but that didn't matter. If you play the bass and are willing to show up, most festivals and music schools are so hard pressed to find enough basses for their orchestras, that not only will you be accepted right away, they'll also pay your tuition and travel. In fact, during the first three years of my bass playing career I didn't even own my own bass; but this was not a problem, as the student orchestras, summer camps, and festivals I played in all provided instruments for me to play, completely for free.

I am willing to bet that, had I applied, I would have been accepted to just about any Ivy League school of my choosing, simply by writing "I play the bass" on my application.

This free and easy aspect of bass playing does change a little bit when you turn professional, at least in larger cities. But the bass players who do in fact become motivated enough to turn pro, and maybe even get jobs in big orchestras, are all still drawn from the same pool of originally passive reluctant draftees, so the culture of bass sections tends to be very different from the other sections of the orchestra. While I can only comment on the bass sections I played in, the attitude we always had could be summed up as, "this thing is pretty much impossible to play, we're doing the best we can, and we didn't really want to be here anyway, so don't bother us with your prissy nitpicking."

Glossary of Musical Terms

BOOP SMEEP MUSIC

A catch-all phrase referring to highly atonal modern music, so named because these pieces all begin the same way: they start with one low note (BOOP), followed by one very high and dissonant note (SMEEP). These two notes are then followed by a mass of harmonically and rhythmically shapeless notes. (This patternless rumbling can go on for anywhere from three minutes to an hour and a half.) The main problem with this kind of music is that, since it lacks any perceivable form or even an occasional melody (and is usually full of senseless dramatic pauses), it is very difficult for the audience to know when it's over. When it seems like the piece has probably ended, there is always a lengthy, pregnant pause where everyone is torn between wanting to clap to celebrate the fact that it's finally over, and not wanting to clap prematurely for fear of looking stupid. Fortunately, the composer usually attends this first (and last) performance of the work, and when the piece ends, he/she will obligingly yell "Bravo!" in the awkward should-I-clap-now silence, letting everyone know it's safe to politely applaud.

CLAM

A really obvious wrong note, usually played by a brass player.

EMOTIONAL TENURE

The fervent (but baseless) belief that you are certain to be hired again for a freelance gig.

HACKOSO

The opposite of "virtuoso," this is a faux-Italian version of the word "hack," and refers to a player who has mediocre technique. The vocabulary of classical music traditionally uses mostly Italian words (such as fortissimo, etc.), so the "Italianization" of English words is common in orchestral culture. Musicians will often put Italian suffixes, especially "-issimo," on English words to make a sarcastic comment, such as, "That really sucked-issimo."

LONG SONG

A piece of music that is at least three hours long, or feels like it. This includes the longer Tchaikovsky ballets, Handel's *Messiah*, Bach's *Christmas Oratorio* and *St. Matthew Passion*, and any Bruckner symphony. Usually stated immediately after the performance, with a long drawn out sighing pronunciation, e.g., "THAT . . . was a LOOOOOONG SOOOONG."

NOTEFEST

A piece of music that has an unusually large number of notes in it. Most Mendelssohn symphonies and Schubert's *Symphony No. 9* fall into this category. Playing these pieces in concert often feels like taking an aerobics class while dressed in formal attire.

TOO MANY SHOWS

Usually said to you after you make an obvious mistake. This is a statement that means "You've been working a lot in the theater district as a pit musician, and while you have been making more money than the rest of us, your technique is suffering because you're spending too much time playing the relatively easy music of Broadway shows." Condescension masked as sympathy.

TOXIC HUMILITY

The belief that, no matter how good you are, and no matter how much or how hard you practice, you still stink.

Thumb Position

I spent three summers playing in the high school orchestra program at Tanglewood. For those of you who may not know, Tanglewood is the summer home of the Boston Symphony Orchestra. It's a big country estate where they have several concert halls. Along with all the BSO concerts, Tanglewood is also home to the Berkshire Music Center and the Boston University Tanglewood Institute, which are summer school programs for college and high school age musicians. Every summer there are hundred of students at Tanglewood, but there are no dormitories for them on the Tanglewood campus. Instead, the students who come for the summer are housed in the dormitories of various local private boarding schools, and some of these schools are three or four miles away from Tanglewood.

There was a shuttle bus that would take all us students from the various dorms to the Tanglewood campus and back again, but we seldom waited for the bus. Instead, we would just go out to the main road and hitch a ride. And believe it or not, very often, I would go hitchhiking with a string bass. You would think this would be a tremendous handicap, but in fact the opposite was true. More often than not, someone (who had driven right past the trumpet players who were trying to thumb a ride) would pull up next to me in a Volkswagen Beetle and, thinking it would be a good joke, say, "If you can get that thing in here, I'll give you a ride. Ha ha ha." What they didn't know was that VW Beetles were tailor-made for hauling string basses. You just flip the passenger seat forward and slide the bass in the back seat, then lift it up to rest on the back shelf, then put the scroll on the dashboard. This method worked, not just with VW beetles, but with just about every two-door vehicle; they were actually much easier to deal with than bigger four-door cars. Sometimes the neck would have to stick out the passenger-side window, but on sunny summer days that was no problem. And away we would go. I usually got rides before anyone else.

One evening I had to go to Tanglewood to pick up my bass and bring it back to the dorm. I took my bow with me to advertise that I was in fact a music student. A very nice middle-aged couple stopped and picked me up. We got to chatting, and I mentioned that I was on my way to get my bass and I would have to hitch a ride to carry it back to my dorm. Without any prodding from me, they very graciously offered to wait in the parking lot and give me (and my bass) a lift back to my dorm. This was like manna from heaven, as it meant I didn't have to haul the bass out to the road and stand there in the dark waiting for a ride. They waited for me as promised, and took me right to my dorm's front door. And I will never forget what they said when we bid each other goodnight:

"We just wanted you to know that there are *some* nice people from New Jersey."

And a One and a Two

People often ask me, "Just exactly what does the conductor do?" I often hesitate to answer, partly because of the complexity of the answer, but mostly because the answer is not at all what people assume the answer will be.

Conductors do many things, not the least of which is picking the pieces of music that are going to be played. This aspect of conducting is often overlooked, but it is one of the most important things a conductor does. I have seen many conductors who had all the personality and glamour you could ask for, along with wonderful musical ability, a fabulous tailor, the works . . . but they had a penchant for some style of music or composer (like Arnold Schoenberg or Charles Ives) that doomed them to a career of academic obscurity.

Besides picking the music, another big part of the conductor's job is picking who plays in the orchestra. While a conductor can alter the sound of an orchestra to be more to his taste by coaching in rehearsal, the easiest way to build the overall sound of an orchestra is to pick players who already play the way you want, so you don't have to do a lot of explaining and retrofitting. It's sort of like the president picking Supreme Court justices, as once a musician is picked to play in a major orchestra, they will very likely stay in that orchestra for their entire 40+ year career. The classic "sound" of a major orchestra has a lot to do with who the conductor picks to be in an orchestra over his tenure, which can be as much as 20+ years of auditioning. Understanding what makes someone a good ensemble player—as opposed to just being able to play a great solo in an audition—is a very important conductor skill.

Depending on the orchestra, conductors are also often responsible for all sorts of non-musical stuff like administration, fund-raising, and public relations. But having said all that, when people ask me what the conductor does, I assume they are referring to what a conductor does on the podium with baton in hand, so that's the question I will answer.

First, let me address some common presuppositions. The mythology of orchestral conducting varies from person to person, but given how conductors are so aggressively "packaged," it is easy for the average layperson to assume that whenever the orchestra is playing, the conductor is in complete command and control, and the power and beauty of the music is all somehow flowing magically out from him. Supposedly, the orchestra is his instrument, and with each player eagerly awaiting his every instruction, the conductor plays the orchestra, not with some bothersome menial technical approach, but instead with pure music, as expressed in his graceful balletic physical motions. Without the conductor's commanding and inspiring presence, and especially without his non-stop waving of the baton to point out where every single beat is, the orchestra would become a leaderless mob, losing all focus and discipline, helplessly disintegrating into soulless rhythmic and artistic anarchy.

Well, that's one version anyway.

Conductors can certainly affect the sound of an orchestra, but "control" is really not the word to use. "Influence" would be better. Like any chief executive, conductors set the overall tone but they don't do very much of the actual work. It's much more of a collaborative effort than most people have been led to believe.

Now it is true that the conductor gets to say when things start. The official process consists of them giving what are known as two "preparatory beats." Their next "down" beat is (in theory) the moment when the orchestra comes in. Seems simple enough, but a very complex series of musical events takes place within that narrow window of time between his prep beats and the moment when the orchestra actually plays. This is all largely invisible to the audience, and here is how it really works:

When a conductor gives prep beats and a downbeat—contrary to popular belief—no one in the orchestra blindly responds. Instead, the prep beats and downbeat are more like the start of a huge game of chicken. No one wants to be the first one to play, so once the conductor has indicated these somewhat imprecise points in time (i.e., the prep beats and the downbeat), the orchestra takes a half-second to come to a consensus on what tempo the conductor has in mind. We compare his request (as best as we can make it out) to the standard way the piece is supposed to be played, and if his indication seems like a reasonable instruction, we will play at the tempo we think he wants us to. On the other hand, if his prep beats make no sense, we will just politely ignore him and play the piece in a standard middle-of-the-road sort of way. In either case, in that split second before the orchestra plays, everyone on the stage pays very close attention to everyone else on the stage, making whatever last-minute adjustments are necessary for 90 people to play that first note at the exact same instant. This happens so often that it is taken for granted, but it really is quite a remarkable bit of team togetherness. The conductor is not "controlling" this. In fact, from his perspective, the orchestra is playing almost a full beat behind what he just indicated, because it takes that much time for the orchestra to collate all the data, come to a decision, and come out of the silence and play all those instruments together in perfect rhythmic sync.

Once a piece of music starts, many people believe that the orchestra needs the conductor's non-stop stick-waving as a sort of visual metronome to keep the orchestra together. But with professional orchestras, this is seldom the case. In hard-core professional orchestras, the beat lies not within the conductor, but within the orchestra itself. Better conductors know this, and they take great advantage of it by swirling the baton around in very vague artistic ways so as not to interfere with the orchestra's intrinsic rhythmic sense. This is harder than it sounds; in the midst of all that dancing and swirling, it is very important to avoid doing anything that the orchestra will interpret as an actual instruction for a rhythmic change, as this can really gum up the works.

One of the biggest problems with many conductors is that, if they have had any actual experience conducting an orchestra (and you would be surprised at just how many of them have not), that experience was gained at the helm of a student or civic orchestra. Now in that sort of environment, the conductor necessarily becomes the center of attention; he or she has to do a lot of instructing, and the players are usually in need of, and are eager to listen to, lots of guidance from the podium. But when you are talking about a major symphony orchestra, things are very different. For those who are new to it, it can be a bit of a shock.

In a major orchestra, the players are all so skilled and experienced that they aren't dependent upon the conductor for very much of anything. And they are generally very assertive, if not downright aggressive, in their approach to playing. For the neophyte conductor in this situation, "leading" is not so much like urging a pony to greater effort as it is like hanging on for dear life while riding Seabiscuit in the back stretch of the Preakness.

This is not to say that the conductor is totally extraneous. In a weird sort of musical symbiosis, the players are playing, not for themselves or for the audience, but for the conductor. And if the conductor shows the proper appreciation for the orchestra's efforts, all is well in the world. However, if they do *not* show proper appreciation, things can get ugly in a hurry. One of the worst things that can happen is when a conductor commits the cardinal sin of saying . . . "watch me."

A conductor who utters this taboo phrase to a bunch of hard-bitten professional musicians is admitting out loud that 1) they have no awareness of how professional orchestral playing really works, and 2) they lack proper respect and appreciation for the skill of the players. To punish any conductor foolish enough to say such a thing, we *will* watch them. We will follow every single twitch without question, and without regard to musical sense or unit cohesion. This of course always results in the whole thing sounding like garbage. Conductors who find themselves in this situation will invariably panic and revert to the only fix they know, which is to demand that the orchestra watch them *more*—to which the orchestra will respond by continuing to play wretchedly, while silently replying "we ARE watching you (tee hee hee)."

A conductor can certainly have some effect on timing here and there. But their direct control is somewhat limited because once a piece has begun, there is only so much attention the orchestra can give to him—after all, most of the time we have to look at the notes on the page. We can see the conductor in our peripheral vision, but the only time we really look up at him is to get his input when there is a big change in the tempo. At those sections, musicians actually make markings in their parts that look like a little pair of eyeglasses. This marking literally means, "The tempo is going to change—look at the conductor." But again, at the point of change, the orchestra does not blindly follow the conductor's motions; we simply use them as a guideline and come as close as we can to our best guess as to what he wants us to do (within the bounds of tradition and good taste), without losing unit cohesion. Also, once we have played a piece for a conductor two or three times, we know how he wants the tempo changes to go, so looking at him becomes less and less necessary.

But all these little technical discussions regarding the waving of a little white stick don't really get to the heart of the question. So let me further explore the symbiotic relationship between conductor and orchestra by first asking this question: why on earth do people practice? Why did the players of a major symphony orchestra devote their lives to perfecting their musical skills to such an extraordinary degree?

Well, here is the answer: human beings have two basic needs. One is to belong, and the other is to be listened to. Playing in an orchestra promises a marvelous fulfillment of those two basic needs in a major way.

So here's the trick: most conductors, being human, also have the exact same human needs to belong and to be listened to; but when directing a major orchestra, this is in conflict with their primary role. Their job is not to perform, but to inspire higher performance in others. To do this, the conductor must transcend their own need to be listened to, and instead focus on meeting the "listen-to-me" need of the players. If a conductor does not do this, you have, in essence, two positive poles of a battery in place. You have a situation where everyone wants to be heard, but no one is doing any listening. This makes it hard for the energy to flow out from the people who are actually playing the notes.

Professional orchestral musicians have put an enormous amount of effort into honing their skills. They did this because they have a really intense need to be listened to. That is their primary motivation, and they are very aware of whether or not a conductor is listening to them. So every time a conductor stands up and says, "everyone listen to me," . . . oi. That's it. Game over. The opportunity for a great performance is immediately lost. Act interested, get the check, go home.

Just for a moment, consider the people who constantly demand that you listen to them and obey them. Now shift gears and think about those few wonderful people you know who accept you, appreciate you, and listen to you.

You probably give the minimum required effort to the former, and your best effort to the latter. Understanding this basic rule of human nature is essential to anyone who wishes to effectively manage top performers, in music or any other profession.

*   *   *

Orchestras were invented in renaissance Italy, and the monarchy "management model" of that era—i.e., one guy having all the power and everyone else having none—is still alive and well in orchestral culture. Because conductors possess such a high degree of at least titular power, they have become a sort of faux royalty. As a result, they fascinate us the same way real royalty does (especially in America, where we have no other royalty to turn to).

Of course, the power and privileges bestowed upon this class of musical royalty make it incumbent upon conductors to *act* like royalty. A conductor's "persona" is a big part of what they do, and great amounts of time and effort are devoted to developing this image.

There are many aspects to a conductor's persona, but one of the most important parts of it is his or her name. While this may seem like a random element to the casual observer, I have developed a theory about conductor's names, which I call the "five syllable minimum" rule.

According to my theory, most Americans do not want to listen to a concert conducted by someone with fewer than five syllables in their name. (Seven or eight syllables are even better—there seems to be no upper limit—but five is the minimum.) Arturo Toscanini, Serge Koussevitzky, and Leopold Stokowski were of course all great names for conductors.

However, if your name doesn't have five or more syllables, all is not lost. You can go the added middle name route—such as Harry Ellis Dickson or Michael Tilson Thomas, and that is generally good enough to get by.

If you can't muster five syllables that way, there are two important exceptions to the five syllable rule: One is "the rule of z's and v's," and the other is "the variable 's' exception."

Simply stated, you can get away with fewer than five syllables if your name contains a "z" or a "v". (Ideally, you should try to have *both* a "z" *and* a "v", *and* have more than five syllables, like, say, Vladimir Ashkenazy. But if you can't quite manage that, you can still get by with just a "z" or a "v".) Zubin Mehta, Fritz Reiner, Lorin Maazel, George Szell, Franz Welser-Möst, André Prévin, Colin Davis, and James Levine are all notable examples of less-than-five-syllable names still attaining great success via the rule of z's and v's.

For the variable "s" exception, if you are under five syllables and there are no "z's" or "v's" in your name, this is okay if there is an "s" in your name that is not pronounced like an "s". Kurt Masur and Charles Dutoit are good examples, or even better, George Solti.

It's also helpful if you can muster up a title somewhere, like the "Sir" in Sir Neville Marriner (although, since he has both five syllables *and* a "v," the "Sir" is not truly necessary). First names that are not pronounced the way they are spelled—like Serge (when pronounced Sair-GAY) or Geoffrey (when pronounced Jeffery) also win points.

(Incidentally, in case you are curious, the current record holder for the most syllables is Rafael Frühbeck de Burgos. Let's face it, with a name like that, he must be absolutely fantastic.)

These are not hard and fast rules. Four syllables are plenty if you have some actual talent. The main thing to remember is, a conductor cannot have the same name as someone you grew up with in Toledo. I would just as soon listen to a concert conducted by Bob Jones or Frank Johnson as I would drink a domestic beer with my hors d'oeuvres of fromage Camembert and pate de foie gras.

*   *   *

There is a famous story about Arturo Toscanini and the NBC Symphony Orchestra, and I repeat it here on a hearsay basis only.

I of course never played for Toscanini, but by all accounts he commanded a great deal of respect from the members of the orchestra. Anyway, as the story goes, Toscanini had some vacation time coming, so he took a week off, and a terribly famous guest conductor from Europe was brought in to conduct the NBC Symphony in Toscanini's place. The program featured a Mozart symphony, and this guest conductor had an interpretive style that was different from Toscanini's. It took quite a bit of doing—three rehearsals at least—for this guest conductor to wheedle and cajole and convince the NBC Symphony players to play this symphony in this different style.

At the dress rehearsal, the guest conductor finally succeeded in getting his way, and the orchestra was at last playing the piece the way he wanted. But then some of the players started to elbow each other. One by one, they realized that Toscanini, who was supposed to be out of town, was sitting in the back row of the hall.

That was it. Despite the best efforts of the guest conductor, the orchestra (to a man), went right back to playing the piece the way they always played it for Toscanini.

Two for the Road

One of the best conductors I ever played for wasn't even a real conductor, at least not in the usual sense. His name was Henry Mancini. Surely you have heard of him—he wrote *Moon River*, *Charade*, and *The Pink Panther*, just to name a few of his many hit movie tunes.

Henry Mancini was not only one of the best musicians I have ever worked with, he was also one of the nicest and most charming people I have ever met. The orchestra just adored him.

The first time I ever played for him was in a Pops concert in Symphony Hall. The program was made up entirely of music he had written. In the rehearsal, we were running through various pieces, and we eventually came to *The Theme from the Pink Panther*. At this point, Mancini just looked at us very nonchalantly and said, "You all know this, don't you?" We all nodded and said "yes." He smiled and said "fine," turned the sheet music over, and we went on to rehearse the next piece on the program.

There was a tremendous amount of "stuff" that occurred in this seemingly simple non-event. You see, it was one thing for us to not rehearse something we had already played many times before. It was quite another thing to completely skip over something that *none* of us had ever played before. Even at Pops, this was highly unusual. So that night, when it came time to play that piece, the intensity within the orchestra was just extraordinary. This man, who we all admired so much, had placed his trust in us, and there was absolutely no way that we were going to let him down. In all my years of playing I have never seen an orchestra so totally focused on playing a piece of music as we were at that moment. With no rehearsal, it sounded absolutely wonderful.

A few years later, the Esplanade Pops Orchestra went on what was to be forever remembered as "The Mancini Tour." The Esplanade Pops had only recently been formed, and many of the players were recent graduates of the many music schools in Boston; the average age was about 25. Most of us had never been on a two-week national Pops tour before.

And what a tour it was. The tour was sponsored by E.F. Hutton, back when people listened when they talked. There was a guy from E.F. Hutton assigned to the tour, and as near as we could tell his only job was to make sure we were all having a good time. Whenever he was in the bar after the concert, all our drinks were paid for, and he would chastise hotel management if they didn't take especially good care of us. One of the best things about that tour was the "hospitality table" that was set up backstage at every concert. At first we thought maybe this was just an opening night party thing, but after the third night we began to realize that they were going to put this magnificent spread out for us every night. So we all quickly learned to skip dinner and just eat backstage. It was grand.

The food was great, but the best part of that tour was the concerts themselves. Mancini's music is so romantic, and he had such a gift for melody. We would play all of his greatest hits—like *Peter Gunn, Pink Panther, Charade,* and *Victor Victoria.* Then we would end the night with *Two for the Road, Days of Wine and Roses*, and a big finish of *Moon River.* The audience was enthralled every night, and so were we.

One of the few non-Mancini pieces on the program was *Chariots of Fire.* In this arrangement, the violins would play the theme once or twice, and then Mancini would sit down at the piano and play the theme himself. But every time he played it, he would alter the melody, creating a "minor" feel on the last triplet of the theme.

One night, near the end of the tour, one of my fellow bass players decided to have some fun. He went around to all the violin parts and re-wrote them so that when the violins played the theme the second time, *they* would play the last triplet with a minor key feel. He let the violins know he had done this, and everyone agreed it would be a great little practical joke.

The concert was going along, and when we got to that point in the music, the violins played the altered notes. Mancini heard this, and he immediately knew that 90 people had conspired to play this little musical joke on him. We were in an arena, with the audience seated all around us, including seats behind the orchestra, so Mancini had to do his best to keep on conducting while trying to keep a straight face. No one in the audience knew what was going on, but we all did. It was a great moment. To top it off, right after hearing this change in the notes, Mancini had to sit down for the piano solo and come up with something else on the spot. Being the master musician that he was, he pulled it off beautifully, and that is even more impressive given the fact that he was also holding back so much laughter.

*   *   *

For the entire "Mancini Tour," the only encore that we had in the books was David Rose's *The Stripper*. Once we played this piece for an encore, if there was any time left, we would just play it *again*. Unusual programming, but the crowd always loved it. To help things along, the bass section figured out a spot in the tune where we would spin the basses, which made it even more of a crowd pleaser.

One night, near the end of the tour (somewhere in Iowa), we were playing in yet another hockey rink, which meant we were completely surrounded by the audience in a big oval. We got to the end and there was plenty of time left, so Mancini came out and we started to play *The Stripper* as the encore. Since the tour was almost over, I decided to have some fun. I turned to the audience that was seated directly behind me (a group of about a thousand people) and I made some motions for them to pay close attention, and "look at me." When the big bass spin came, since this section had been alerted, they reacted with a big round of applause. I then gave them a little hand signal to stop, and, en mass, about a thousand people stopped clapping.

I turned around, and Mancini was looking right at me. He was truly amused and he was smiling, but the look on his face also said, "What the hell are you doing?"

I just shrugged and pretended to know nothing. The crowd behind me could see all this and they got a big kick out of it.

So we finished the piece and, as Mancini walked off stage, he looked at the other bass players and said, as a joke, "Where's he working tomorrow night?"

There was still some time left, so Mancini came back out and we started to play *The Stripper* one more time. This time the audience behind me was really primed and pumped, and I started to get their attention again with little hand signals, all hidden behind my bass.

When we came to the grand "spin spot," instead of spinning, this time all seven of us lifted our basses over our heads and shook them. This inspired an even more massive outburst of applause from the section directly behind me, which I cut off a bar later with a quick hidden hand movement.

At this point the rest of the audience had caught on that something was going on between me, the audience section behind me, and Mancini. Mancini started to pretend to be upset at this apparent loss of control, crossing his arms, looking at the audience and motioning to me. It was all improvised, and he played it up beautifully.

When this piece (and the concert) ended, Mancini didn't even turn around to face the audience. Instead, he walked right across the front of the stage, took me by the hand, and gave me a personal bow. 20,000 people gave me a huge round of applause.

That moment was the high point of my entire bass playing career. Henry Mancini. What a classy guy.

*   *   *

Another symphonic urban legend:

There was once a young conductor who arrived at the concert hall one evening only to realize that he had left his baton at home.   Horrified, shocked, and panicked, he called the orchestra's personnel manager over to him and said, "I'm afraid we will have to announce that the concert will be delayed, I have to run home and get my baton."

But the manager replied, "Oh, I don't think that will be necessary."   The manager then turned around to the many musicians who were unpacking their instruments backstage and announced, "I'm afraid the conductor has forgotten to bring his baton." On hearing this, 30 of the musicians reached into their cases, and collectively pulled out 30 batons.

The Esplanade

One time-honored Pops tradition I always enjoyed was the mid-summer week of free concerts on the Esplanade—which is where the name "Boston Pops Esplanade Orchestra" comes from. As I mentioned before, the Esplanade is a park that runs along the Charles River. Arthur Fiedler had the idea of playing free concerts out there way back in 1929. Everyone told him he was nuts, but he did it anyway, and it's been going on ever since. The Pops plays in the Hatch Memorial Shell, which was built specifically for Pops concerts.

The Hatch Memorial Shell was recently refurbished, but when I was there it was a true antiquity. Whenever it rained, and sometimes when it didn't, there would be a long puddle in front of half of the downstairs lockers. The place was locked up tight nine months out of the year, so dust would collect all that time—not that you would really notice, as the backstage area hadn't been cleaned since Eisenhower was president. You had to be careful not to brush your white tux coat up against the walls. There was an old electric organ back there (probably installed in 1939 when the place was built), that ran on vacuum tubes; it actually worked. Despite the recent renovations, directly behind the back wall of the Shell, there is still the same old originally-installed 12-inch-wide rickety retractable metal staircase that shakes violently back and forth as you carefully negotiate it to descend from backstage to the locker level. (OSHA would certainly not approve.) On the stage itself, there are various light fixtures that are home to thousands of overfed spiders, who feast on the hordes of bugs that fly around the entire Shell every night. On the sides, there are floodlights at floor level that are designed to create a beautiful lighting effect on the semi-circles of wood that vault over the stage—looks great from the audience, but on a 90-degree Fourth of July, the last thing you want is a bunch of heat lamps shining point blank onto your black tux pants.

Our seven bass trunks were all placed in a small alcove stage right. They just barely fit in this little room, and it was so small you couldn't open all of the trunks at the same time, because the lids would slam into each other. It always looked like King Tut's tomb in there, with the dim lighting and all those sarcophagus-like trunks up against the walls. There was no room for anyone or anything else in that alcove, so it was our little space.

When I first started playing Pops, there was a grand old gent named Frank Gallagher, who was the bass section leader. On the last night of each Pops season, he would buy two bottles of champagne at Symphony Hall's backstage bar and we would all drink an end-of-season toast.

Well, the way the schedule worked out one year, the last night of the Pops season was not in Symphony Hall, but on the Esplanade. Unfortunately, there is no bar backstage on the Esplanade, but old Frank would not be deterred, and showed up with a cooler filled with iced-down champagne. At intermission we went backstage to our little King Tut Tomb space and had a final end-of-season drink amidst the heat, bugs, and occasional feral cat.

That gave me an idea. In the Hall we were terribly pampered, as we had a full restaurant and bar for our intermission dining and drinking pleasure. But when we came out to play a week of concerts on the Esplanade, well, putting up with the heat and the bugs *and* having no refreshments was just unacceptable. So the following summer I suggested that, there being seven nights and seven bass players, we should each take a night to bring refreshments.

I can't remember who took the first night—it must have been me—but that first night someone brought seven cold beers in a cooler and some nice little hors d'oeuvres. Musicians being somewhat competitive by nature, the next night the next guy brought some very fancy imported beer and fresh lobster. The next night, well, it just went on and on; it became a fantastic game of culinary one-upmanship that resulted in a fabulous intermission feast every night.

When it came time for Frank's night, he brought marinated swordfish wrapped in aluminum foil. He wanted to heat it up, so he also brought along . . . a butane blowtorch. I am not exactly sure what was up with this particular blowtorch but when Frank lit it up and put its flame against the foil, it turned into a small flame thrower. So there we were, backstage with only a 10 minute intermission, and there was Frank in his white tux trying to heat this stuff up. Flames were shooting out everywhere in this old wooden structure. We all pleaded with him to stop but he paid no attention. I thought for sure we were going to burn the place down.

The intermission bass section party in the Hatch Shell was so successful that we did it on every single Esplanade night every year after that. Over the years an amazing array of appetizers and exotic libations came through that little alcove. Of course, being just as competitive as everyone else, every year I always tried to outdo the other bass players on my nights. One year I brought a blender, along with some frozen strawberries and tequila, and I managed to whip up and serve seven frozen margaritas under the most primitive conditions imaginable (I was lucky to find an outlet with AC current). The best part was, with only nine minutes of intermission, I had moved over to the bass alcove so fast, I had the blender up and running just as a lot of musicians from other sections were filing out past us. They all looked at us with great envy and amazement. But I think I reached my zenith one year when I decided to do something truly bold and outrageous. After we played the first half of the concert, everyone went rushing backstage to see what I had brought. There, in the bass alcove, were several white pizza boxes, and when we opened them up, you could see that they were steaming hot.

"How did you keep them hot?" one amazed fellow bass player asked me.

With more than a little smug pride, I answered, "I had them delivered." I had called a pizza joint on Charles Street for a delivery at 8:30 p.m., and I had given Angelo, the Hatch Shell Manager, the money to pay the delivery guy. The smell of the pizzas had been occasionally wafting into the shell during the first part of the show, but I was the only one who knew where the aroma of pizza sauce was coming from. Appropriately enough, that night we had been playing Mendelssohn's *Italian Symphony*.

The Fans Closest to Me

On the Fourth of July, the buses carrying the musicians would always leave Symphony Hall an hour before show time, complete with a police motorcycle escort to get us down to the Esplanade . . . which, I have to say, was pretty cool. The motorcycle cops would take turns leapfrogging ahead, stopping traffic at all the intersections, letting us run the red lights. Trouble was, the early departure time (15 minutes earlier than usual), combined with the police escort, would get us there in less than 10 minutes, which meant we had 50 minutes to kill in the sticky heat before show time.

As much as I loved playing concerts on the Esplanade, in that 50 minutes there was literally nothing to do except maybe practice, and I wasn't about to do that. So out of sheer boredom, one Fourth of July I put on my white tux and wandered out to the front of the audience area. Splayed out in front of me was an amazing assemblage of refugee humanity: people standing, lying, and sitting every which way, on chaise lounges, under tents, and on blankets. They all looked like they had been out in the sun a little too long—which they had. Eventually I caught the eye of this guy standing at the front and said:

"If you don't mind my asking . . . I mean, it's none of my business, but . . . there are 250,000 people here. How in the world did you manage to be in the front row??"

He proceeded to explain to me that this was an annual family tradition, and all these people in his extended family would camp out on the Esplanade for *two weeks* so they could be in the front row on the Fourth of July.

I was utterly amazed—and vastly complimented—that anyone would go through so much to hear me play. And I told him so. We got to chatting, and he introduced me to everyone in his family. There were something like 30 of them out there.

From their perspective, I was probably the first "official" person to see these people as anything other than pests and a bother, and they were absolutely delighted that someone from the orchestra was actually talking to them. The next thing I knew, I was invited to dinner. I hopped over the crowd control barrier, sat down on their blanket, and oh my gosh, what a spread these people had laid out!

For the rest of the week I had dinner each night with my new-found fan club. We had a grand old time.

At last, that week of concerts came to an end. We played the last piece on the last program, and the applause started to die down. The concertmaster got the signal from the personnel manager to leave the stage, and as soon as he took his first step, the orchestra began its usual mad dash to get onto the buses. At that moment, my pals in the front row—all 30 of them—yelled out in unison: "All-right-Jus-tin!"

On the bus back to Symphony Hall I received a tremendous

amount of ribbing about this from my colleagues—"So, your family here tonight?" I didn't know what to say. Oh well . . . I didn't give it much thought after that, and neither did anyone else.

A year rolled around, and there we all were again, playing yet another week of concerts on the Esplanade, and sure enough, there in the front row were the same 30 people, all camped out as usual. The first night, the concert ended, the applause died down, and over the post-applause silence came yet another chant from 30 distant voices, floating up to the stage: "All-right-Jus-tin."

In something so pecking-order oriented as an orchestra, having your own personal cheering section is a major breach of protocol. So the following night I went down, chatted with them, ate a few cookies, thanked them for the accolades, and asked kindly if they would tone it down. "Great, no problem," they said. The concert ended. The applause died down. "All-right-Jus-tin."

Well, like anything else that at first seems to have no point, if you do it often enough, it becomes an institution. And Justin's fan club gradually became an accepted phenomenon. I was always in a race at the end of show to see if I could get off the stage before they would do their little cheer for me.

The strange thing was, for many years after I left the Pops, whenever I ran into one of my former Pops colleagues, they always would tell me, "Ya know, your Esplanade fan club still cheers for you every night."

*　　*　　*

In 1986, the Pops broke a long time tradition of playing on the Esplanade on the Fourth of July, and instead flew down to New Jersey to play a live TV show to celebrate the centennial of the Statue of Liberty.

At the rehearsal, someone came out and told us that, at the start of the show that night, we were going to play "in sync" with a recording of *The Star Spangled Banner*. No explanation was given. We said nothing, but we all thought this was very strange. "We aren't some lip-syncing pop singer, we're the Pops, we can play this piece by ourselves," we all muttered. But in orchestras, you do what you're told. So we practiced playing along with the tape. Music minus one orchestra.

When the show started, they played this recording of *The Star Spangled Banner*, and we started to play along. And then our questions were answered: out of the sky, flying right over the orchestra at about a thousand feet, came two F-16 fighter jets. It is truly unbelievable how loud these things are. We couldn't hear a thing over that roar, not the tape of the music, not even our own instruments. There was no way we could have played it on our own.

If I Practiced, I Could Be Really Good

I never auditioned to get into the Pops. My bass teacher knew the personnel manager, so when the "other" Pops orchestra was put together for the first time, I got a phone call: "Wanna play Pops?" Sure. Woody Allen was right, 80% of success is showing up, and I showed up. With one recommendation and one phone call, I was "on the list"—for 18 years.

However, if one wishes to get a tenured position in a major symphony orchestra, one must win an audition. Auditions are the most stressful experiences I have ever been through. If I had a choice between taking an audition and being detained by the Turkish police, I would take the Turkish police.

Auditions begin by reading the classified ads in the union newspaper. If an orchestra has an opening for an instrument, they place an ad saying when the auditions will be held, along with general information about how much the job pays, and so on. If you see an ad for your instrument, and you're feeling ambitious or masochistic or both, you write to the personnel office. They write back with the date and time of your audition, along with "the list"—i.e., a list of the pieces of music that you will be asked to play at the audition.

Every audition requires you to play a solo. Sometimes you get to pick your own, and sometimes they pick it. In a bass audition, if they pick it, it's usually a movement from a Bach *Cello Suite*. Next, you have to be ready to play "excerpts" from various pieces in the standard repertoire.

The word "excerpts" means one thing in most common usage. In the orchestra world, it means something very different. It is a hateful little word that refers to famous little sections for your instrument's part in various pieces of symphonic music. And these little sections of music, these . . . excerpts . . . are extremely hard to play (if not downright impossible). They are the musical versions of tongue twisters. You spend much of your student years figuring out how to play them, and then you memorize them, and then you ponder how you are going to play them while under the extreme stress of an audition. I have known musicians who spent every waking moment thinking about excerpts. They practiced them constantly. Excerpts became their life.

The most common bass excerpts asked for in auditions are from Strauss' *Ein Heldenleben* and *Don Juan*, Beethoven's 5th and 9th; and Mozart's 35th and 40th Symphonies. But that's just the beginning. There are lots of other nasty little excerpts to choose from, and every instrument has its own unique list of orchestral excerpts that are required at every audition.

For some auditions, they will tell you exactly which excerpts they expect you to play. But in most auditions, they won't tell you that. This means you have to be ready to play *any* excerpt from *any* piece that's on "the list," not just the famous ones. This adds an enormous amount of work to your preparation. I have seen some audition lists where they included almost every piece in the concert repertoire, with no specific excerpts named.

I don't want to sound like I'm whining, but gee whiz, this is *hard music*, folks, just page after page after page of really nasty stuff. To be ready to play every note of it perfectly is, well, I don't know how people do it. I certainly couldn't.

So once you get "the list," you have a few months to get ready. You practice and practice. At last the big day comes, and you get yourself to the city where the audition is taking place.

At this point you have invested years and years in acquiring technique, as well as the cost of lessons, school, and your instrument. On top of that, now you have also invested almost every waking hour for the past three months learning and polishing this audition repertoire —not to mention the cost of two plane tickets for yourself and your bass, plus cab fare and your hotel.

The night before, your mind constantly runs through all the pieces you have been practicing. There are always one or two spots that keep you up at night, because if they ask for them, you know you're not as ready on them as you should be. It's so frustrating because you've been asked to prepare two hour's worth of material—maybe more—but you're only going to play for about a minute or two. So which minute will it be? You hope you guessed right, and that you focused your time on the right excerpts, because you can't possibly learn all of it as well as you would like to. Then your mind leaps ahead. What if I win? My whole life will change, I'll have to move to a new city and start a whole new life. What if I lose? You try not to think about that.

Now, just to give you an idea of the amount of competition involved, consider this: a major orchestra like the Boston Symphony Orchestra has about eight bass players who each stay in the orchestra for about 35 years. That means that, on average, there is an opening in the bass section of a major orchestra like the BSO about once every four years. But in Boston alone, along with a long list of local freelancers who are subbing in the BSO, there are three large music schools (and several smaller ones) that collectively spit out at least two orchestras' worth of young, eager musicians—including maybe 10 or 20 bass players—every year. And that's only the local competition. An audition for a spot in a major orchestra like the BSO also attracts just about every recent graduate of every music school in the country, not to mention all the guys who are already playing professionally in smaller regional orchestras. That doesn't include the guys who are already in a major orchestra bass section in another city but want to move somewhere else.

The upshot of all this musical math is, when you get to the audition, it's a sight to behold. There, in every nook and cranny of the concert hall basement, are bass players. They are everywhere, like roaches in a tenement. You might see 200 of them or more, and like roaches, for every one you see there are two that you don't. There are tall, skinny bass players with tall skinny basses, and short fat bass players with short fat basses. All of them are practicing, running through all those same nasty excerpts that you've been working on for months, and every one of them, it seems, is playing them a whole lot better than you.

Someone from management comes around and, in a very impersonal fashion, tells you where to go and exactly when you'll audition. You warm up; you try to get your nerves calm. Eventually the moment comes, your name is tersely called, and you are taken away from that cacophonous nether region of rumbling bass excerpts. Gradually you get nearer and nearer to the terrifying silence of the stage.

Most auditions are held behind a screen, presumably to keep it fair and impartial. Sometimes they will even put down a carpet so the committee can't tell if you're male or female by the sound of your footsteps. The fact that you cannot see who you are playing for makes it an even more impersonal environment.

At this point the adrenaline is pumping so hard through your system that you feel as though you have no control over your hands, and so on top of the shaking, you're sweating too, making everything slip. Presumably, there is a committee on the other side of the screen but of course you can't see them. The personnel manager is your only human contact in this otherwise empty, lifeless void of a concert hall stage. It is a completely new and unfamiliar acoustic environment and you have no time to get used to it. You are a nameless invisible commodity, and you are alone.

At last, the great mystery is revealed, and you see what music you have to play. The manager puts the music in front of you, and says, "Play this," so you play. "Now play this . . ." and you play. "Now play this." You play. All those hundreds of hours of work and effort are boiled down to these two minutes of playing. No second chances. And every note you play is sucked up into the sonic vacuum of the concert hall.

At last this eternity ends, and the manager says, "Thanks very much," although you never hear those words. All you can hear are the voices in your head arguing over which mistakes you may have made and what you should have done differently. And then, you don't leave, you retreat. You go downstairs and pack up. And then you wait.

Eventually, someone comes around to where you and maybe five other bass players are waiting for the results. In most cases you are told, rather curtly, that nobody made it. The end. In my career I took five auditions for five major orchestras. I never made it past the first round in any of them.

If you do in fact make it past the first round, you have to come back a week later and go through it all again. Even if you are the one who wins, that's not necessarily the end. Sometimes they will have you play in the orchestra for a few weeks or months to see if you work and play well with others. Some orchestras require that you submit to a psychiatric exam. (To win an audition, I think it actually helps if you're a little crazy.) And even after all that auditioning, at the end of it all, if the conductor just doesn't like you, he can peremptorily veto the whole thing and the process just starts all over again.

As much as I pity those who take auditions, I also have pity in my heart for those members of an orchestra who have to sit on those audition committees and listen—carefully—to bass player after bass player, playing the same three pieces of music over and over for hours on end.

The high stress, extreme competition, and demanded perfection of auditions is something all professional musicians must go through, and this commonly shared emotional trauma is a big part of musician culture. It is the reason for one form of terribly cruel musician humor: in a Pops rehearsal, when someone is playing an exposed solo passage, no matter how much of their heart and soul they may have put into playing it, if they make just the slightest little error, someone in the orchestra will inevitably call out:

"Thank you. NEXT!"

Shot from Guns

One summer we were playing a Pops concert on a big estate somewhere on Long Island. As usual, we were going to play the *1812 Overture,* with fireworks and cannons. As we were rehearsing, way way out in the stage left grass we could see a series of army trucks driving up, towing the 105mm howitzers that would be fired that evening.

Oh yeah, cannons for *1812*, big deal. We had seen cannons so many times that we paid them no mind. So we finished the rehearsal, and started killing time before dinner.

There wasn't a whole lot to do except walk around this old estate. As I walked, I could hear the occasional BOOM of the cannons; I guess they had to practice just like everyone else. I was bored and a little curious, plus I was in my white tuxedo so I was feeling bold. I wandered up to these National Guardsmen and their cannons, and I started chatting with them. I had never talked to an artilleryman before, so I was intrigued. They were bored too, so they gave me a little tour of the gun, the sight, and how it worked.

I couldn't resist. "So guys, whaddaya say, can I fire off a round?"

They got a big kick out of this and said, "Well, no, you can't fire an actual charge, but we'll let you pull the laniard on an empty chamber."

So these guys went through this whole rigmarole of sighting the gun and checking the bore to make sure it wasn't loaded, and it was all this really cool military talk, but finally they were ready to fire so they handed me this rope and I pulled on it. It wasn't like firing off a real charge but it made a very satisfying "clunk" on the firing pin nevertheless. And then they all laughed at me. "I don't get it, what's so funny?" I asked. "Well," they said, "if you had fired a real round standing where you're standing, the recoil would have broken your leg."

I guess it's not good to play with howitzers unless you know what you're doing.

Then I asked these guys, "Hey, these guns are pretty loud, how do you manage to not go deaf firing them?"

And they said, "Well, we have these nifty little earplugs, but really, the noise isn't so bad behind the gun. Out in front of it is where it's really loud."

As they said this, I looked down the barrel of the gun and there, less than 100 yards away, was the bandstand where I would be sitting and playing that night.

"But," I said, "*I'm* going to be in front of the guns tonight."

"Yeah, you are," they said, breaking into evil laughter that made me shudder with foreboding.

I had played many a Pops concert with howitzers before this

particular concert, but this was the first time that the guns in question had been pointed right at the stage, and I was plenty worried. Not sure what else to do, when we started to play the *1812 Overture*, I took some Kleenex, wadded it up as best I could, and stuffed it in my ears. I was glad I did, because when the moment came in the piece for the cannons to be fired, well, there we all were, in the direct line of fire. It's kind of hard to explain just how loud a 105 mm howitzer is. The sound is so loud I'm not sure it even qualifies as a sound any more. It's more like a shockwave. It feels as though you are being punched in the chest by someone three times your size, from all directions.

Each concussion actually made my bass jump up a few inches. And everywhere I looked, I saw players in the orchestra covering their ears. After the very first shot, the entire second violin section had surrendered en masse, but amazingly, enough people kept playing that we didn't actually grind to a screeching halt. There aren't many orchestras that will continue playing through an artillery barrage. I was very proud of my colleagues that night.

*   *   *

One summer I was working in the production truck for the annual TV broadcast of the Pops Fourth of July show out on the Esplanade, and some enterprising young camerawoman had placed herself and her camera on a floating dock on the Charles River. The spot she picked was about 40 feet away from the business end of the four howitzer cannons that were there for the *1812 Overture*. Everyone in the truck thought it was a great shot, and indeed it was, but I remembered my Long Island experience and, since I wasn't on headsets, said to the director, "You need to tell Suzie that those guns are really loud."

So the director said to Suzie, "Suzie, we are told the guns are really loud."

"Gotcha," said Suzie. But I could tell from the casual tone of her voice that she hadn't quite captured the meaning behind what I had just said. So this time, loud enough to be heard directly through the director's headset mike, I said:

"Uh . . . those guns are really loud. They are really, *really* loud."

"Gotcha," said Suzie. I could also hear an unspoken "I heard you the first time." Well, things were moving along, I had done my best, and I could do no more for Suzie. It was now a few hours before show time, and someone decided we should tape Suzie's beautiful shot of the cannons for the six o'clock news. Everyone was all set, the tape was rolling, the National Guard artillerymen were ready, and Suzie was ready. I mentioned that the guns were really loud one more time, but I still failed to make an impression.

The order to fire was given, and four 105mm howitzer cannons went off all at once.

BLAMMADABLAMBLAMBLAMBLAM

The TV truck (a huge semi-tractor trailer that was a good 100 feet away) rocked back and forth from the blast. Echoes of the cannon fire, like distant thunder, came bouncing back from neighboring towns in all directions. On the TV monitors, Suzie's shot of the guns was completely obscured by a cloud of gray smoke, which eventually drifted away with the breeze. And then, silence.

"Suzie," said the director, "that was a great shot."

Silence.

"Suzie?"

Silence.

More silence.

"Suzie??"

There was a long pause. Then, over the speakers, we heard a quiet, quivering, plaintive voice that, barely over a whisper, said:

"Holy s**t."

The Last of the Ninth

Every year, the nightly bass section party at the outdoor Esplanade concerts had become more and more competitive. No matter whose turn it was to bring the goodies, during each intermission one of our bass section colleagues would treat us to ever more exotic food and beer from around the globe. One summer, when it was my night to bring seven beers and food, I went into a liquor store and looked for something unusual to bring. I spotted a six-pack of a dark brew called "Molson Brador." I had never seen it before, so I bought seven bottles, put them on ice in a cooler, and brought them down to the Hatch Shell.

The concert started and we played whatever was on the first half—probably a symphony, though I forget which one. Intermission arrived, and everyone scurried over to our little bass alcove to see what Justin had brought to eat and drink. I proudly brought out the seven bottles of this exotic libation.

That summer we had some new guys in the section. They were very young and very pure, just out of conservatory. They were also very eager to belong, so to entertain ourselves, every night we put a fair amount of peer pressure on these guys to chug down a whole beer during the nine minute intermission. It was hot, so it didn't take much prodding. As usual, we all drank our bottle down, and when we heard the tuning "A" being played, we rushed back out on stage.

There is one small detail about all this that I didn't know at the time, but I know it now. Molson Brador was not beer. It was . . . malt liquor. I can't tell you how much more alcohol it had than regular beer, but in retrospect, I would hazard to guess that it was at least three times as much.

Have you ever gotten a little drunk and noticed that the room was starting to spin around you, even though you were standing still? Well, that's what the audience and my music stand started to do. And I was not alone. We were all feeling the effects, and our heretofore teetotaling new young members of the bass section were completely soused.

So the second half of the concert began with a performance of the Hummel *Trumpet Concerto*. Our guest soloist was a local high school student who had won a competition to play a solo with the Pops. Needless to say, he was quite thrilled to be there.

The Hummel *Trumpet Concerto* is not terribly difficult, but there is one little thing about it worth mentioning: the second movement is written in the key of C-flat. For those of you who are not all that musically inclined, well, music is written in different keys, which means some of the notes are played a half step lower. In the key of B-flat, for example, if you see a B or an E, you play them a half step lower, i.e., B-flat and E-flat. That's what the black keys on a piano are for.

This is no big deal, as musicians are used to playing in different keys. Long before you ever get to be a pro, you practice those scales up and down thousands of times. Three flats, four flats, even five flats I can handle without even thinking about it.

But C-flat . . . well, in the key of C-flat, there are *seven* flats. That means every single note on the page is flat, including C and F. C-flat and F-flat are very unusual notes, because C-flat is also B, and F-flat is also E . . . since there are no black keys in between C and B, or F and E. If that's too confusing, never mind, but trust me, this is unusual enough to deal with when you're sober. But, to have to play in C-flat when you've just chugged the equivalent of three beers in nine minutes, well, trying to collate all those lines, dots, stems, flags, and rests into information that has to be sent to your fingers, which have to then press down on exact spots on the fingerboard, and do this in exact rhythm . . . yikes.

Fortunately, this onslaught of flats was in the slow movement, so our seven little befuddled brains were doing reasonably well. Most of the notes were fine. The trouble was, every time we had to play a C-flat or an F-flat, invariably, one of us would play C or F natural. This wasn't so bad by itself, since the audience can't really hear things like that, but when you're in the middle of a string section you can hear everything, and every time one of us goofed on a C-flat or F-flat, it sounded like a rhinoceros that had just eaten several undercooked black bean burritos, and, well, we all just thought that this
. . . was *so* funny.

We tried our best not to laugh, but of course one of us would chuckle, then one by one we would all start guffawing. Then, as soon as we got it back under control, someone else would play another C or F (not flatted) and it would start all over again.

Yet another problem facing us was that, for that summer season, the bass section was placed upstage in the center, rather than off to one side. This meant we were right in the conductor's line of sight. The conductor could see that we were breaking up non-stop. So right there, in the concert, in the middle of this trumpet concerto, he started to yell at us.

"Basses! What are you doing up there? Shut up! Stop fooling around!!"

Our talented young soloist continued to play his trumpet as best he could, looking around with eyes as big as saucers, which seemed to plaintively ask, "*this* is the Boston Pops??"

And we all thought . . . that this was *soooo* funny.

The basses were loaded. It's a wonder we weren't all fired.

*   *   *

There was once a conductor of the Boston Ballet Orchestra who had a very strange laugh. It sounded sort of like "e-heh, e-heh, e-heh." In ballets, the brass players often have to sit there for extended periods with nothing to do except counting rests, so in order to pass the time, these brass players began to imagine that this "e-heh, e-heh, e-heh" was a reference to a person named "Al Heh." This name then evolved from "Al Heh" to "Albert Haahh," and the brass players gradually invested all sorts of powers in this mythical being. "Albert Haahh" gradually became an icon representing the highest aspirations of brass players. If someone played something well, or just did something bold or laudable, the brass players wouldn't say, "Good job." They would just say, "Al Haahh."

"Al Haahh"—or "Albert Haauggghh," as he eventually was named—became a phantom member of the brass community. Whenever we went on a Pops tour, his name would appear on every sign-up sheet for optional activities. And whenever the orchestra was served a meal on a plane, the flight attendants were always trying to find the "Mr. Haauggghh" who had requested the vegetarian kosher low salt meal.

[Editor's note: you can read The Legend of Albert Haahh *at www.justinlocke.com/al.htm.]*

Parts is Parts

There is one terribly important element of every orchestral performance that few outsiders ever think about, and that is the sheet music that's on the music stand in front of each player.

To give you an idea of how much sheet music is required for playing just one piece on a typical orchestra concert:

- There are about 16 first violins (two to a music stand), so that's eight first violin parts;
- Twelve second violins, so that's six second violin parts;
- Eight violas, four parts;
- Eight cellos require four parts as well;
- Seven basses (the odd man at the end gets his own book), also four parts.

So that's 26 string parts.

Then you have, on average: three flutes, three oboes, three clarinets, and three bassoons. They all play their own unique part, so that's another 12 parts.

You'll also typically have four trumpets and four trombones, at least four horns, and a tuba, which makes for 13 more pieces of sheet music.

The percussion section may get five parts, and then there's the harp, the piano, the guitar, and the bass guitar.

So, for each piece of music being played, there are at least 60 different pieces of paper, and each one has to be placed in a specific player's folder.

Maybe that doesn't sound so bad. But wait, there's more.

At the Boston Pops, a typical concert has about 15 pieces on the program. This means that, in total, each concert requires about 900 pieces of paper, and all those pieces of paper have to be in the right folders each night. And remember, there are often extra people on the stage (depending on which piece you're playing), such as vocal soloists, saxophonists, or antiphonal brass players, not to mention narrators and choirs and whatever. Plus, programs change every other night, so every 48 hours those 900 pieces of music have to be removed and put into storage and another 900 pieces have to be very precisely inserted into the folders. And all, and I do mean *all*, of that sheet music has to be there.

The Pops employs three full time librarians to do all this "librarianizing," as I like to call it. During the Pops season, they work constantly. Their families forget what they look like.

The librarians' work is not just about taking the parts of each piece out of their little storage envelope in the library and collating them into each of the 60 folders on the stage. They also check to make sure that each folder has all of its music inserted *in program order*. And if someone like a fourth horn or third clarinet is not playing in a piece on the program, for that folder they will insert a sheet of paper that has that piece's title and the word "TACET"[7] written in *big* letters so that player won't accidentally come crashing in on the downbeat with the notes of the next piece on the program. (Don't think this doesn't happen anyway.)

Also, sometimes a piece on a program will be slightly altered at the last minute—e.g., there might be a four bar "cut," or maybe a different ending. If this happens, every single one of the 60 or so parts of a given piece has to be carefully marked, by hand, with the new cut or addition. And they have to be 100% correct, because just one mistake in one part can mean, at best, loss of precious, rare, expensive rehearsal time, and at worst, a train wreck during a concert.

The Boston Pops library is on the third floor, and it runs about half the length of Symphony Hall, with cabinet after cabinet filled with tens of thousands of parts for all the arrangements that have been created specifically for the Pops over the years. Its entrance is right next to the stage, so that if there's a problem, the conductor—and the orchestra—will all yell "BILLLL!" (Bill Shisler that is, one of the Pops librarians), and he'll hear his name reverberating through the beautiful acoustics and come down to fix the problem.

When the Pops goes on tour, the librarians come along too. They bring their own trunks that contain all the sheet music (and if the trunk with the sheet music doesn't make it to the show, there is no show), as well as their own mobile collection of library tools—paper cutters, tape, post-it notes, binding

---

[7]Tacet: a common (Italian) musical term originally meaning "silent." To an English speaking musician, it means "You don't play this entire piece."

tools, and all sorts of hardware specifically designed for repairing music. During the week on the Esplanade, they even bring along a full-sized copying machine.

After each program has been played, each folder is quickly gathered up from the stage and taken back to the library, where all that sheet music has to be slowly "un-collated" out of the players' folders and put back into their little files. Keeping track of it all, well, I don't know how they do it sometimes.

And on top of all that work with the folders, there is a steady stream of people coming into the library before and after every rehearsal and every concert with some niggling little special request for a copy of a practice part for a piece that's for a concert a month away. On more than one occasion the librarians have allowed me to photocopy a bunch of Tchaikovsky parts for some personal project, at no charge.

I have a very fond place in my heart for the Pops librarians. They are under enormous pressure, they put up with so much from every angle, their work is never done, and they never get any applause.

Name That Tune

When you play in a professional orchestra, you have to maintain a certain degree of emotional detachment, otherwise the sheer power of the music on top of the job pressure will overwhelm you. So you make a lot of bad jokes and play little games to take your mind off things.

To give you an example, there is a game that professional musicians play with their sheet music. The idea is to take a sincere and/or artsy title of a piece of music and alter it into something humorous, usually with a cynical or salacious slant.

While I say "humorous," I feel compelled to warn you that this particular kind of musical humor is very much of an "I guess you had to be there" kind of thing. Most of these little title changes aren't that funny all by themselves. But when you are in the glorious confines of Symphony Hall, with everyone in the audience dressed in their Sunday-go-to-meetin' clothes and the entire orchestra is wearing formal attire, and you open the folder on your music stand knowing that you must now face the challenge of playing a whole bunch of nasty notes in some overly elegant, and perhaps slightly pretentious, hoity-toity piece of music, and there on your sheet music you see some bit

117

of graffiti scrawled by a colleague that captures all the angst, cynicism, and general perversity that is so common to orchestral musicians, the humor is much-needed relief. These sick little attempts at humor are so incongruous that, when read in the elegant environment of a concert, it is virtually impossible not to get a fit of the giggles. Some of the altered titles scrawled on your sheet music can be 40, 50, or even 60 years old or more (the librarians never bother to erase them), and yet when you read them you can feel a true sense of oneness with some poor colleague, probably long since dead, who was once in the same spot you are in now—trying to have a little fun in the midst of the soldierly boredom and stress that is so often the lot of the orchestral musician. I suppose some classical music lovers will find such humor to be blasphemous, but I think that people who have devoted their entire lives to playing classical music have earned the right to make a joke about it once in a while. So here goes.

Ideally, you should be able to turn a syrupy sentimental title into something derisive or obscene by adding or deleting as few letters as possible (extra credit is awarded if you do it by changing, adding, or deleting just one letter) . Other than that rule, the standards are pretty low. Any sick joke, cynical statement, or sexual reference is acceptable, because the extreme anxiety of the job will make you laugh at just about anything. Some title changes of classical music are found in orchestras everywhere, and most musicians know them already, but for the uninitiated here are a few examples.

Back in 1880 a composer named Max Bruch wrote a piece for violin and orchestra titled *Scottish Fantasy* (its official title is *Fantasy for Violin and Orchestra and Harp, Freely Using Scottish Folk Melodies, in E-flat Major, Op.46*—yeesh). Because of the large number of fast little notes the violin soloist must play, instead of *Scottish Fantasy*, musicians will almost always refer to it as *Scratch Frantically*.

Way back around 1800 or so, Ludwig von Beethoven wrote his only opera, *Fidelio*. It's about a guy named Fidelio, who is actually a girl named Leonore. I think. Who knows, it's an opera, so maybe it's the other way around. Anyway, since the lead is a cross-dresser of sorts, in a fine bit of political correctness, the opera is named for one sexual personality (Fidelio), and the overture is named for the other (Leonore). To complicate matters, Beethoven wrote several different versions of the overture, three of which are titled (no surprise here): *Leonore Overture #1, Leonore Overture #2,* and *Leonore Overture #3*. Overtures to famous operas are often played on symphony concerts, and so with apologies to all the Beethoven worshipers out there, in a professional orchestra, it's not uncommon to open your part to the *Leonore Overture #3* and see that the title has been changed to *Le Snore Overture #3*.

Somewhere around 1900, a French composer named Claude Debussy wrote some pieces for solo piano. One of these was his famous *Claire de Lune* (which is French for "moonlight"). While pianists will generally leave titles alone, when this piece is arranged for orchestra, in virtually every part on the stage, the title will be re-written as *Clear the Salune*.

Along with those, there are some other title changes that are also fairly commonplace—Offenbach's *Orpheus in the Underworld* is always re-written as *Orpheus in his Underwear*. Another classic: back in 1874, a Russian composer named Modest Mussorgsky wrote a suite of pieces for solo piano, and titled it *Pictures at an Exhibition*. In 1922, these piano pieces were arranged for orchestra by Maurice Ravel. But instead of the original title, if you were to go up on the stage you would see that in almost every orchestra part, instead of *Pictures at an Exhibition*, the title will be re-written as *Pictures of an Exhibitionist*.

As you can see, the humor in many of these title changes relies solely upon their depravity, so good taste prevents me from giving you a complete list. However, here are just two examples that I think I can slip past the censor:

In addition to *Claire de Lune*, Claude Debussy wrote a piece for orchestra called *La Mer* (*The Sea*). But in just about any orchestra, at least in the bass parts, you will usually find that the title has been changed to another French phrase—*La Merde*.

One night I was playing a concert somewhere, and the program included Dvorak's *Carnival Overture*. In a delightfully artistic twist, the title had been reworked ever-so-slightly, to become Dvorak's *Carnival Knowledge Overture*.

Of course the kitschy titles of pop music pieces provide endless opportunities for this kind of musician humor. Just two common examples: *I'm in the Mood for Love* is always re-written as *I'm in the Nood for Love*, and *I've Grown Accustomed to Her Face* will always be changed to *I've Thrown a Custard in her Face*.

On one Pops tour, we played a medley of "train" melodies, which included *Take the A Train, Chattanooga Choo-Choo,* and *Orange Blossom Special*. This arrangement, which was actually kind of fun, was originally titled *All Aboard*. But since we had to play it night after night on a two week tour, by the end of the tour, you could see the title re-written in every single part as *All RBoard*.

I was always eager to contribute to this unique literary genre. My best effort, I think, was when I took the title of my Pops bass part to *New York, New York* and converted it to

Nyork Nyork Nyork–
Hey Moe Hey Larry Wait for Me.

There is another variation of this unique art form, where a title won't be changed at all; instead, someone will write a pithy comment underneath it. For example, during a recent Holiday Pops concert, I happened to see a bass part to the well-known Christmas carol, *Do You Hear What I Hear*. Orchestral playing is, of course, all about matching pitch and rhythm with your fellow musicians, so I thought it quite amusing to see, underneath the printed title of *Do You Hear What I Hear*, this neatly penciled-in subtitle:

Apparently Not.

*   *   *

One of the nice things about Boston Symphony Orchestra sheet music parts is that, in general, they have been extensively used before you ever get to them.   Old, used parts are always wonderfully marked up with all sorts of warnings and bowings and other bits of information that make playing a piece that much safer and easier. These markings were usually written by some poor slob who, eons ago, came in wrong in that same piece and so felt compelled to write something like a sharp or a flat or perhaps the word "COUNT!!" in the part to let himself—and now you—know there's some sort of musical trap to watch out for. Some of the parts of the "light classics" in the library have the look and feel of genuine antiques—I'm sure some of the parts in the library date back to the founding of the BSO back in the 19th century. Why buy new ones? It's not like the notes of a Strauss Waltz have ever changed.

Suffering for One's Art

Before you ever get to a professional orchestra job, you must go through a lengthy apprenticeship that usually starts in grade school. Along with all the lessons and youth orchestras, one of the many rites of passage for young musicians is going to a summer music "camp."

When I was 15 years old I saw a brochure for the National Music Camp, which is generally just known as Interlochen. One photo in the brochure really made an impression on me: there was a semi-circle of high-school-aged girls, each one of them playing a harp, sitting in a grove of pine trees next to a lake. I just fell in love with that picture and all that my adolescent imagination read into it. I sent in my application in record time. Being a bass player, I was of course accepted right away.

Interlochen is a remarkable place. Every summer, thousands of kids from age nine through college descend upon this musical Shangri-la. There they have a vast array of performing arts ensembles as well as classes of all types in music, dance, drama, art . . . you name it. For eight solid weeks, in this idyllic northern Michigan environment between two beautiful lakes, you are constantly exposed to music, art, dance, and theater, and all day long you can hear Tchaikovsky and Bach wafting out of practice rooms and concert halls.

However, I wouldn't want you to suffer any pangs of envy stemming from not getting to go yourself, so let me tell you about this experience in a little more detail.

As I said, my overly-active adolescent imagination had created a lot of preconceived notions, so when I arrived at Interlochen, the reality of it was a bit of a shock. It's probably my own fault for not reading the brochure more carefully; I confess, I had not really looked much beyond that photo of the nymphets playing harps by the lake. I honestly thought that upon my arrival I was going to be ensconced in the loving arms of the many muses of the arts—not to mention the arms of the harp-playing nymphets. Instead, much to my surprise, I discovered that I had joined the army.

We lived in cabins (that is, barracks), with about 20 boys in each. This being a music camp, there was no shortage of trumpet players, so each morning started bright and early with reveille. We would get one little warning blast on a trumpet. Two minutes later the real one would come, and we had to throw on a pair of shorts and line up on the tennis courts for calisthenics. Then we had to come back to our cabin and scrub it down from top to bottom. Then, and I kid you not, we had inspection, with demerits awarded for poorly made beds or a less than pristine shower stall. Then we got into our uniforms. For boys, these were blue corduroy pants (not shorts), and heavy cotton blue shirts—in July.

"Where are all the beautiful nymphets with the longing looks, playing harps amidst the pines?" I wondered as I scoured the toilet. I couldn't find them anywhere.

I gradually deduced that the only possible location of the much-sought-after nymphets was over a mile away, in a legendary wooded glade often spoken of in hushed tones but never actually seen, known as the High School Girls' Division. Here, so saith the legend, hundreds of nymphets frolicked freely in their blue corduroy knickers and light blue knee socks. But alas, I was separated from my objects of desire not only by this considerable distance, but also by a 12-foot high chain link fence (which very well may have been electrified) and a phalanx of humorless counselor guards who stood jealous watch over their ambrosial charges 24 hours a day.

Everyone, including the staff, had to wear uniforms at Interlochen. But in spite of the social equality implied by the uniforms, I encountered a very definite class distinction: there were kids whose parents had coughed up the full tuition fee, and then . . . there were the scholarship kids. If you were there on a scholarship, this obligated you to do two things. First, if you played an instrument that could be played in both the orchestras and the concert bands (a band is sort of like an orchestra but has all wind and brass instruments), you had to play in both ensembles. Since bands don't call for string sections, all of the violinists, violists, and cellists from across the tracks were gleefully unaffected by this little requirement, but concert bands call for one string bass. So, being one of the two bass players on scholarship that summer, I was obligated to spend a total of five hours each day in rehearsal: orchestra in the morning, band in the afternoon. (On top of that, being the idiot I was at that age, with my one remaining option for another class or activity, I opted for bass lessons, which meant I was going to spend one helluva lot of time playing the bass, and nothing else.)

The second requirement for scholarship kids like me was that you had to work an hour a day. This didn't sound so bad—the brochures and applications said this would be something simple, like filing papers in an air conditioned office or handing out programs at concerts. But they didn't say positively. I'm not sure how my work situation came about. It may have had something to do with my typical lack of organization regarding paperwork, which resulted in my applying late for a scholarship. In any event, my work assignment was not at all what I expected.

For me, there was to be no handing out programs, no cushy office work, no filing of papers, nor any conditioning. Instead, I was assigned to be the janitor of the junior girls' division, a section of the camp for girls aged 9-12. Six days a week, right after lunch, under a hot noonday sun, in my camp uniform of a heavy blue shirt and full length corduroy pants, I had to sweep sand off sidewalks for an hour. On rainy days I would go inside where it was hotter still and kill spiders. "Where are the nymphets?" I kept asking myself.

Aside from all the daily scut work, one of the most memorable parts of my Interlochen experience was their tradition known as "challenges," which applied to everyone, scholarship or no. It was a diabolically efficient system designed to motivate us to practice. Here's how it worked: once each week, the basses would all line up in the bass hut, and the bass teacher would select a passage for us to play, taken from the music of that week's program. (Of course we had no idea what the passage would be, so we had to practice everything. I told you it was diabolical.) The first chair kid would play this excerpt, and then the second chair kid would play it. Then the entire section would vote on who they thought was better. If a majority thought the second chair kid was better, the two of them switched places. Then the third chair player would "challenge" the just-demoted-to-second-chair player, and so on down the line. Like any audition, or any other situation of being judged by your peer group, this was just unbelievably stressful, and it went on every single week, for players of all instruments.

There were two high school orchestras. One was called "The World Youth Symphony" and the other was called "The High School Concert Orchestra." Guess which one was better. The trouble was, if you wanted to make the leap from the second orchestra to the first orchestra, not only did you have to practice enough to get to the first chair spot in the second orchestra, but you also had to know the music the first orchestra was playing to be able to challenge the last chair player of that orchestra the next day, which essentially doubled your practice time. That whole summer I was right on that razor's edge, always first or second chair of the second orchestra, but never quite making it into the first orchestra. I also tried to challenge into the first band every week, to no avail. At least I made the other bass player who was there on scholarship practice his band music. Misery loves company.

Well, I got my money's worth (as I learned a lot that summer), but I have to say, my best day at Interlochen was my last day, and not just because my ongoing misery of scrubbing and sweeping and challenges had ended.

Camp had officially ended on a Sunday night, and early Monday morning everyone was packing up and getting ready to board buses for points south. I was on my way to eat breakfast, when, for the first time that whole summer, one of the high school girls actually came up to me and started to talk to me in a friendly manner.

No matter that she needed someone to shlep her 200-pound

steamer trunk from her cabin to the parking lot and I was the only guy she could find who was big enough and dumb enough to do it. This was a real live girl, and she was talking to me. I was in heaven.

I agreed to help her and the next thing I knew, I was doing the impossible: I was entering the High School Girls' Division. I know some will scoff and say this could never happen. No one (and certainly not a geeky kid like me) would ever be allowed to enter that mythical forbidden city of delight. But on this day, now that camp was officially over, the garrison of counselor guards that usually manned the gates was nowhere in sight; they were all packing up to go home like everyone else. So in I went.

This young lady brought me to a spot near her cabin and said, "Wait here," and then she went inside to get her gear. As I stood there in the early morning sunlight waiting for her, I happened to glance up at my surroundings. Imagine my sudden and total amazement when, through the large un-curtained windows of all the cabins, I could see all these high school girls . . . rising out of their bunks . . . languorously yawning and stretching . . . in the nude.

At last, at last, I had found the nymphets I had so earnestly been seeking!

I admit, they weren't playing harps in a grove of pine trees down by the lake, but you can't have everything.

The Black Sea

There is a very old joke about a guy who goes up to a stranger in New York City and asks, "How do I get to Carnegie Hall?" The stranger's response: "Practice, man, practice."

To those who have never done it, I suppose the process of learning to play a musical instrument must seem rather mysterious. Civilians often ask the question, "How many hours a day do you practice?" implying that all that matters is how much *time* you spend practicing. Yes, it is important to invest a fair amount of time, but there are actually different kinds of practicing. There is "development of core technique" practicing, there is practicing of specific pieces of music, and there is "maintenance" practicing, where you are not trying to learn or improve anything, you're just keeping yourself in shape. There is an awful lot to it, and I have never seen anyone write about it, so here is a little introduction to that mystical Zen world of practicing a musical instrument. Bear in mind, everyone has a different approach, so I can only tell you how *I* got to Carnegie Hall—and my approach to playing the bass was extremely unorthodox, to say the least.

I think most people who pick up an instrument start out the same way (at least, this is how I started): their goal is to achieve the satisfaction of "playing a tune." Technical exercises are not very much fun to play, so most folks will pick out a piece and play it through from start to finish. Or at least try to. When I was a beginner, whenever I got to a spot that was "iffy," well, I might repeat that section a few times to try and "get it."

This form of "practicing" is fun for beginners, but in the long run it is terribly inefficient. Playing a tune over and over again only improves your ability to play that particular tune. When you try to play a different tune, well, other than those parts of it that are identical to the tunes you have previously learned, you're pretty much starting from scratch. And here is something that no one ever tells you: if you *practice* badly, instead of improving yourself, you are actually training yourself to *play* badly. The bad habits and incorrect technique get ground in like stains in the carpet, and they become that much harder to fix later on.

When I was in high school, I was a member of that large society of musicians whose "technique" had come about rather haphazardly from this process of simply learning various disparate "tunes" and orchestra parts. I had a lot of enthusiasm, and I suppose I had some "talent," but solid technique, no. And while this was enough to make me a big high school star in Toledo, when I came to Boston I found myself facing the very sudden, and very distressing, conclusion that in this brave new musical world my "technique," such as it was, was woefully inadequate.

I think in every musician's life there comes a crossroads where you have to decide if you are going to do this just for fun, or you are going to take it on as a sort of religious calling. This was my moment. At this point I was fortunate enough to meet up with a violinist named Joseph Scheer (who is the current concertmaster of the Esplanade Pops Orchestra). When I expressed a desire to improve myself, he impressed upon me the need to practice fundamentals—that is, scales and arpeggios.

(Quick definitions here for non-musicians: A scale is a series of adjacent notes. If you start on "C" on a piano keyboard, and play each white key in a row up to the "C" an octave higher, that's a C major scale. It goes C-D-E-F-G-A-B-C. Now go back, but this time skip some notes, and just play C-E-G-C. When played all at once, C-E-G-C is a C major chord. When you play the notes of a chord one at a time, right after another, it's called a "broken chord," or an "arpeggio.")

The reason scales and arpeggios are so important is that almost all of the music a string player plays is made up of them. If you have two notes in a melody that are a step apart, well, that means those two notes are a part of a scale. If you already know the locations and fingerings of *all* the notes of *all* the scales, then you should be able to play any two adjacent notes in any piece of music without thinking about it very much, since you have already learned them as part of a scale. If the notes are *not* adjacent, it's essentially the same deal, except that those notes are all parts of an arpeggio. In theory (very much in theory), on a string instrument, if you can play any scale or arpeggio, you should be able to play any piece of music written for your instrument, since all of the notes of any piece are merely bits and pieces of these patterns—i.e., scales and arpeggios—that you already know. It's similar to being able to read a new book because you already know all the individual words.

That first year at the New England Conservatory had left me much humbled, but also much determined. When the school year ended, I went back to the family farm in Ohio, and I played scales and arpeggios for eight hours every single day, for three solid hot summer months. My poor family. You have to be pretty motivated to play scales and arpeggios for eight hours a day, because it is boring as all hell. But my ego was hurting, so I was motivated.

That summer of fundamentals was a watershed experience. That autumn, when I came back for my sophomore year, my bass teacher was much impressed with my improvement, so much so that he recommended me to a local orchestra contractor. Two months later I was playing my first real, paying gig. All those hours and hours of playing nothing but scales and arpeggios had paid off. They had transformed me from a somewhat promising student into a professional. I was 19 years old; at that point I decided I didn't need music school any more, and I dropped out. (With honors. I'm not making that up.)

Since I had improved so much by practicing these fundamentals, about a year later I decided to see if there might be a way to boost my technique still further by finding and practicing an even deeper level of fundamentals.

Bear in mind, a bass, unlike a guitar, is a "fretless" instrument, which means you have to be able to find the notes on the black sea of an ebony fingerboard, and you can't be off by more than a couple of millimeters. In this barren unmarked wilderness, you must navigate using only two reference points: first there is the "nut" at the top of the fingerboard (where the strings go through a notch and into the peg box), and the second is the base of the neck (basses are built so that, when your thumb hits the base of the neck, your index finger is right at "D" on the G string). In the most basic level of bass technique, the way you locate the first note you want to play is by bumping your hand against one of these two points and then measuring the distance, by "feel," to the note you want.

I decided that I wanted to be able to find *any* note on the bass with absolute pinpoint accuracy (and lightning speed) from either of these two reference points. But that was just the beginning. I didn't want to have to use those reference points any more than absolutely necessary, since bumping them in order to find a note might add extra steps, and therefore slow things down. I wanted to be able to find any note, not just from these two reference points, but also while starting from *any other* note—with no guesswork or prayer involved. And I wanted to be able to get from any note to any other note not just with total accuracy, but also with the absolute barest minimum of motion, so as to do it faster.

I didn't know it at the time, but I was about to completely unlearn everything I knew about the bass and learn to play it all over again.

On any given evening I would pick a note—say, B-flat—and train my hand to find each of the other 44 notes, starting from that point. The next night, I would start with B-natural, and slowly measure the distance to each of the other 44 notes.

This kind of practicing requires an enormous amount of just agonizingly slow repetition. I would take as much as five or ten seconds—or more—to go from one note to another. I had to do it at that speed because it took that long to ponder all the purely mechanical information that had to be considered. When playing a B-flat, what was the first knuckle of my index finger doing? Am I lifting my fingers up off the strings too high when they aren't in use? Would it help to move my elbow up an inch? Or maybe a millimeter? How is my posture affecting the proceedings? Can I eliminate some excess motion by moving my shoulder forward or backwards a half inch? I took as much time as was necessary to consider every possible aspect of playing each pair of notes. Speed was not important. Total accuracy and total efficiency were everything.

This was incredibly dull work, but what the hell, I was young, I had a lot of energy, and I had nothing else to do. During this four month period I did virtually nothing else but practice in this manner, measuring these precise distances between notes. I lived on roasted peanuts and grapefruit juice. Each day became a process of deep meditation. My whole concept of time and space was altered by this experience. I think I saw God a few times. I would practice until the early hours of the morning, then, since I was always too wound up to sleep, I would wander the streets of Boston's Back Bay until the sun came up. I often found myself hallucinating, caught up in a strange euphoria usually only experienced by tribal medicine men.

I could go on at length about all the mechanical aspects of playing a string instrument—for example, how you hold your hand in a "position," and all that goes into "shifting" from one part of the fingerboard to another, and then there's all the stuff you have to learn about using the bow. It is easy to become obsessed with the mechanical aspect of playing all by itself. But at some point you have to pick your head up out of all this musical engineering and attempt to transcend the physical dimension of the process. You have to start thinking about something else entirely—that is, what exactly is it that you wish to "express" with all this new-found technical ability?

In my miasma of farm boy ignorance I had developed the

assumption that if one could play all of the notes on an instrument with great ease and accuracy, this would, by default, instantly make one a great "artist." But, much to my chagrin, I found this was not the case. Being able to play a lot of notes doesn't make one an "artist" any more than having a big vocabulary makes one a poet. After all that work, I was shocked to discover that instead of being finished, my study of the musical arts had only just begun.

While one never truly breaks free of the physical challenges of playing a musical instrument, at that point in my musical career, they had become much less of an issue. Instead of worrying about mechanical issues, I found myself delving ever deeper into this mystical art we call music. I still spend enormous amounts of time every day thinking about how to achieve greater connection to the hearts and souls of the people in an audience, and pondering how subtle shadings of time and tone can express and evoke different emotions. It has been a never ending process of analysis and discovery.

And compared to all that, I have to say, finding the locations of 45 notes on a fingerboard was relatively easy.

*   *   *

One of the most interesting things I learned from my periods of intense eight-hours-a-day practicing had to do with the workings of the subconscious mind, and its role in the proceedings of learning to play an instrument. You can practice something for days and days and still not get it. So you give up. But a week later you try the same sequence of notes again and voilà, it's right there. Much to my amazement, all this super-slow, super-accurate practicing paid dividends for years afterward, because my technique seemed to magically improve without any practicing at all. I had trained myself that severely and efficiently, and it took that long to assimilate the effects. Of course I had to play enough to keep my hand strength up and keep calluses in shape, but other than that and prepping for auditions, I never felt a need to practice again. My hands and fingers just "knew" where all the notes were, and that knowledge has never left me. I had such a clear mental picture of where the notes are and what I had to do to measure each interval that I could practice without having a bass in my hands. I could just look at a bass part and do the calculations in my head. I haven't touched a bass in 10 years and I still know where every note is, within a couple of millimeters. I have never had to "remind myself" of where they are; it is all burned in there permanently.

Successful as this system was, there was one downside to this unorthodox approach. Most of my colleagues were all great believers in needing to practice every day. For them, practicing was a sort of daily religious ritual, a requirement for membership in the exclusive society of professional classical musicians. Trouble is, I am a pragmatist. I am lazy. And I *hate* practicing, so I didn't want to do it any more than was absolutely necessary. Also, let's face it, the majority of bass parts just aren't that hard to play. And as far as tone production, when you're talking about the bass in the real world, no one really cares about it. They just want you to play loud.

As my disdain for daily practicing became known, I came to be looked upon by my colleagues as a sort of musical heretic. My professional reputation suffered, because most people assumed that I couldn't be very good (even if I was once), since I didn't practice every single day.

So whenever I played next to someone who knew me only by my slovenly reputation, they would always be amazed at my ability to hammer out a bunch of nasty little sixteenth notes with total accuracy when called upon to do so. "How can you play all those notes without practicing?" they would ask in amazement.

"Why should I practice?" I would reply. "The notes are always in the same place."

On the Road Again

One of the best "perks" of playing in an orchestra like the Pops is the travel—assuming of course, that you like to travel.

Whenever the Pops plays outside Symphony Hall—be it across the street at the Marriott Ballroom or across the Pacific in Suntory Hall—it is a marvel of logistical organization. All the cellos, basses, and big percussion instruments have their own specially designed travel trunks. Cello trunks are enormous square boxes, and bass trunks are even bigger—seven feet high, about three feet across, with lots of padding inside and special straps designed to hold your instrument without scratching the finish.

One of the nicest things about doing Pops concerts outside the Hall was that, unlike your typical freelance gig, you didn't have to shlep a string bass anywhere. Whenever a tour was imminent, all you had to do was take your instrument down to the basement of Symphony Hall, put it in a bass trunk, and then stick some masking tape on it, upon which you would write your name, where you were going, and the date. That was it. Your bass trunk would magically appear backstage at the concert venue, whether it was in Ohio or Osaka. Hopefully, you remembered to pack your bow.

When the Pops travels, there are more than just bass and cello trunks. There are horn trunks, violin trunks, and trumpet trunks, which hold about ten instruments each. This saves everyone from carrying all those individual instruments onto the plane.

Tours with the Pops are fun, but they are brutal. Every single day you get up, pack, have a hurried breakfast, pay your hotel bill, get on a bus, ride the bus, get off the bus and onto a plane, ride the plane, get off the plane and get onto a bus. Then you ride the bus, get off the bus, check into a hotel, and get in line with 100 other people to get into one of the two hotel elevators. If you're lucky, you have an hour to take a nap. (If you're luckier still, the person in the room next to yours isn't practicing for an upcoming audition.) Then you grab a quick dinner and catch yet another bus to the show that night. After playing a concert for 20,000 cheering fans, you take yet another bus back to the hotel. At this point you're too wound up to sleep, so you hang out in the bar until closing. Then you do it all over again the next day. And the next. And the next.

Pops tours are always very well planned. Something so complex has to be. Everyone is given a little yellow booklet with the tour itinerary, telling you exactly where you have to be and when. There is always one management person who travels to the next city a day ahead of the group to make sure the hotel is ready. Before all the new airline security issues took hold, it used to be that you would pack your luggage in the morning and just leave it outside your hotel room. A porter would pick it up and you didn't see it again until you arrived in the next city, where it would be delivered right to your room. That was nice. Sometimes we would travel on charter flights, and that meant we didn't have to go through the terminal at all; the buses would roll right onto the tarmac next to the plane and up you go.

When you get to the concert hall, one of the managers has been there long before you ever arrived, and, like Hansel and Gretel's breadcrumbs, they have posted signs everywhere backstage, with arrows pointing the way to dressing rooms, instrument trunks, wardrobe trunks, stage left and right, bathrooms, refreshments. . . everything.

When on tour, as soon as the concert ended there was always a rush to get out of the venue and back to the hotel as quickly as possible. Part of the reason for this was that the instrument trunks and everything else all had to be loaded onto a truck, which had to travel all night to get to the next venue in time for tomorrow night's show. The main reason we wanted to get out, though, was that hotel rooms, bars, saunas and pools are just a whole lot more fun than the concrete perdition backstage at an arena.

To speed things up, we bass players always kept our tuxedos in our bass trunks. The rest of the orchestra could store their concert clothes in wardrobe trunks that were placed in dressing rooms, but rather than do all that running around backstage, the bass players would just change clothes wherever the trunks were . . . although now that the section is co-ed I don't know if things have changed. Probably not.

One night we were performing at the Wolf Trap Center near Washington, D.C. The main stage at Wolf Trap is huge, so when an orchestra plays there, walls of a smaller concert hall "shell" are lowered into place. Our bass trunks were all placed directly behind the back wall of this shell by the stagehands.

As soon as the concert ended, while the audience was still filing out, we all immediately carried our basses behind the back wall of this concert hall shell and strapped them into their trunks. Then, in our standard end-of-concert mad dash to get to the buses, we started to rip off our tuxedos. Imagine our surprise when we looked up and discovered that the entire back wall of the concert hall shell had just magically and silently flown up into the rafters—and there we were, all seven of us, in our skivvies, in full view of the exiting audience.

*   *   *

On one tour we were on a commercial flight and it had been overbooked by the airline. The ticket agent announced this and asked if anyone was willing to give up their seats in exchange for a free flight. Unbeknownst to the Pops managers, the entire percussion section (being the entrepreneurs they all are) opted for this bonus.   We were well into the flight before the managers found out that the entire percussion section would be on a later flight . . . with a concert at 8 p.m. The managers were a little peeved, to say the least. You can't do a concert missing an entire section of players. What a nightmare. So a new rule went into the Trade Agreement that year: no unauthorized independent travel on tours.

The Trade Agreement requires that every tour must include at least one "free day" a week, and it was always a topic of major planning, discussion, and intense competition as to what people would do on their free day while on tour. It's supposed to be a day to recuperate from the rigors of traveling but instead it usually became the hardest day of all. On a free day I would usually rent a car and go see the local scenery, and it was not unusual for me (or anyone else) to drive 300 miles or more. In Portland, Oregon, you could either drive up the Columbia River Gorge to Mount Hood or go west through wine country and end up at the ocean. In Sacramento, a drive to Muir woods and San Francisco was typical. In Scottsdale, tubing down a river in the desert was lots of fun. In Orlando, what else? We would all take off for Disneyworld. In big cities like Chicago or Los Angeles, the choices were too many to name here.

There was one group of people—we called them the "Esplaneers"—who had some sort of mountain climbing fetish. They would get up at 3 a.m. on the free day, drive as much as

142

10 hours (if need be) to get to some nearby mountain peak, climb it, climb back down, and drive back in time to get a couple of hours sleep before the next day's flight.

On the day after the free day, there was always a great deal of one-upmanship on the plane ride as we all tried to outdo each other with tales of the outrageous things we had done with the free time. On one tour I had gone to a "warplane" museum at a small airport in Orlando, and as I was leaving I saw a sign next to an old biplane that said, "Go for a ride—$60." So I pulled out my per diem money and next thing I knew I was flying over Orlando in an open cockpit plane just like Eddie Rickenbacker. I won the "best free day adventure" award for that one.

*   *   *

There was one percussionist who really had free day planning down to a fine art. He had a distinct advantage over the rest of us, because he could pack any number of boxes for the tour truck, mark them "drums," and have that box carried along in the tour truck for free. No one questions such things. Any box marked "take on tour" is automatically loaded on the truck.

On one tour to Florida, this percussionist managed to bring along all of his scuba diving equipment– it had been packed in a box marked "soprano tympani" or some such. On another tour that included a free day in Portland, Oregon, he had an empty percussion trunk added to the usual shipment. He marked it something like "fragile– glass wind chimes." On his free day in Portland he purchased several cases of Willamette Valley wine. He then proceeded to pack it all in this percussion case, and it was all carefully shipped back to Boston, for free.

144

*   *   *

One thing I always enjoyed about Pops tours was that, unlike the shows in town where everyone ran home right after, it became a sort of extended camping trip; in our "downtime" we tended to bond together as a group, since we had to depend upon each other for companionship. We would often gather at the hotel bar after the show, and in distant locales like Tokyo, at dinner we would all share our discoveries of fun things we had individually found to do during the day. On the evenings of the free days, John Williams or the tour sponsors would occasionally throw gala dinner parties for us.

While some activities involved everyone, we also often split up into subsets of people who tended to stick together.[8] When on tour it's important to "buddy up" with at least one other person. It's good to have someone you feel comfortable with to sit next to on the buses, since you tend to spend, on average, at least an hour (and more often two hours) on a bus every day. And it's not good to spend that much time next to an empty seat.

I had various tour buddies over the years, but one summer, we had a new face in our midst: a young lady who was with us temporarily as a management intern. She and I just happened to hit it off, and well, the next thing you know we had become tour buddies. When her management responsibilities allowed,

---

[8]A common subset was a foursome of horn players that would play a continuous game of "hearts" to pass the time on the daily plane rides. Of course, consistently getting four seats together on every plane ride required some doing. When we left the hotel in the morning, they would split up and take different buses to the airport. Whoever was on the first bus to arrive could run onto the plane and reserve a whole row of seats.

we would sit next to each other on bus rides, and when there was a free day, since she had no money and no plans, we spent those together too.

Now I can quite honestly say that this was all very innocent and very much on the up and up, but of course, she was young and single and attractive and so tongues began to wag about us. Nothing was going on, but nevertheless we were a hot topic of conversation and speculation.

Well, anyway, the tour ended and we all flew into Boston late one night. This young lady was living in a furnished room not far from my house, so everyone saw us hopping into a cab together. But when we got to her rooming house apartment, there was no one there, and she had no key. "Well," I said, "let's deal with this tomorrow—you can sleep at my place." So she crashed on my couch.

The following morning, since I had been gone for two weeks, I had no food in the house to make breakfast. It being Sunday, we decided to head over to Doyle's, a popular local restaurant, for brunch. We were sitting there having a lovely if exhausted time when, wouldn't you know it, the entire Pops percussion section walked in and saw us sitting there. And I could see this twinkle in each of their eyes that said, "AHA! Now we know."

Denying their suspicions would have only served as more proof to them, so I just looked at my tour buddy and said, "So much for your reputation."

*   *   *

On some Pops tours we traveled on charter planes, which meant that unlike commercial flights, it was just us, and no outsiders on the plane.

Federal regulations require that on every single flight, even on charters, the flight attendants must tell you all the usual instructions of how to use a seatbelt, how to use the oxygen mask, where the exits are, and so on. So even though we had all seen these instructions a hundred times, on every single flight, we, like so many air commuters, had to sit through that safety lecture one more time.

We decided to add our own variation. On each flight, whenever the flight attendants got up to do this little shtick, we would cheer wildly for them. No matter that they were presenting just a simple little pantomime of the same old instructions. We always acted like an extremely rowdy crowd at a burlesque show. When they reached for the orange oxygen mask we would start chanting: "MASK! MASK! MASK! MASK!" When they pointed out the exits we would all point too.

Then we would start to chant "BUCK-LE! BUCK-LE!" And when they demonstrated the tightening of the seat belt, we would all go "OOOOOOH!" When they demonstrated the release of the seatbelt buckle, we would go crazy with cheers and wild applause.

Those poor flight attendants. There was nothing they could do; they were required by federal law to go through the whole routine, so they couldn't stop. They were so used to going through this little demo with no one paying attention, and suddenly they were "on stage," with every little movement eliciting tremendous applause. They were good sports about it though.

It was nice to be in the audience for a change.

Some Flute Player

A typical week of Boston Symphony Orchestra concerts includes a concert on Friday afternoon. Playing the concert in the afternoon allows the symphony players to have a weekend night off. It also means that Symphony Hall is available on Friday nights to be rented by touring orchestras, famous soloists, and so on.

I once had a very busy Friday. I was subbing with the BSO that afternoon, and I had to play a show downtown that same night. Plus, a friend was driving in from the suburbs to meet me for dinner in between concerts; she was to go downtown with me that night to see the show I was playing.

So I played the BSO concert, and right after that I met my friend. We went around the corner and had dinner, and then we had to deal with the logistics of getting ourselves, two cars, and a string bass down to the theater district, where parking is almost impossible.

Then I had a brainstorm. There is a parking lot next to Symphony Hall. It's normally packed with BSO players' cars, but it being Friday night, I figured it would probably be empty. If so, maybe we could ditch her car there and go downtown together. Sounded like a plan.

So I opened the stage door of Symphony Hall, and there I found several of the security people and stagehands sitting around. I asked them, "Would it be all right if my friend left her car in the lot tonight? Is there anything going on tonight that people need the lot for?"

One of the stagehands said, "Oh yeah, go ahead and park. There's just some flute player here tonight."

"Well," I said, "thanks very much." Now bear in mind, at this point I was just trying to be palsy-walsy and jocular, so I said, "I guess there won't be very many people here tonight. I mean, you heard one flute player you heard 'em all, right?"

They all thought this was very funny. Stagehands have a very unimpressed attitude toward all musicians, no matter how famous. "Yeah," they said. "You said it. Some flute player. You heard 'em all. Ha ha ha."

Great. So I ran up to the stage, grabbed my case, and started to pack up my bass for the trip downtown. I was just about finished when I heard a voice behind me, which, in the acoustically perfect environs of Symphony Hall, said:

"Are you the guy who said . . . 'if you heard one flute player, you heard 'em all'?"

I turned around, and there, in the dim light, I saw . . . James Galway (arguably the most famous flute player in the world). In a very ugly mood, I might add.

Have you ever done something in just sort of a kidding way and

150

then suddenly realized that you've done something really, really offensive? So offensive that no amount of apologizing could ever hope to fix it? This was one of those moments.

Well, I had to do something. After some of the fastest thinking I have ever done, I said, "Oh no, Mr. Galway, that wasn't me. That was some other guy."

"Harrumphh," he said.

"And I told him he should buy a ticket and come hear you play tonight because you would really change his mind."

There was an awkward Symphony Hall silence, and then he said, "You sure it wasn't you?"

"No, no, of course not."

"Humph," he said, and walked off. Gee whiz. Just what I needed, the first time I sub with the BSO, to get into a fist fight with James Galway on the stage of Symphony Hall. Me and my big mouth.

Join the Pops, See the World

In 1987, with John Williams conducting, we packed up and went to Japan for two weeks of Pops concerts: three days in Osaka, then ten days in Tokyo.

One of the great things about this tour to Japan, besides just the excitement of it, was that once we got to Tokyo, we didn't have to travel any more. A tour usually involves day after day after day of plane rides, with maybe one or two "free days," but in this case we were playing 10 days in one city, so it felt like we had 10 free days in a row. In Tokyo. We each had our own room in a four-star hotel, all expenses paid. We just had to play a concert for two hours each night for our adoring Japanese fans. Not a problem.

One of the wonderful things about traveling, of course, is seeing how other cultures do things. For example, in Pops concerts at Symphony Hall, the local Boston crowds know that Pops is a fun night, and it often takes a while to get them to settle down and actually listen to the music. In Japan, though, things are quite different.

In concert halls in Japan, the audience files in well before concert time, they sit in their seats, and . . . wait. In total silence. As we came on stage, they would just sit and stare at us. Very different from Symphony Hall, where you can barely hear the orchestra play the first piece, there is so much audience chit chat going on.

One of the pieces we played on that tour was a piece by Leroy Anderson called *The Typewriter*. If you don't know it, well, it's a cute little tune in which a typewriter is played in rhythm to the music. Some orchestras will synthesize the sound of the typewriter with some other percussion instrument, but not at Pops. Amongst the vast collection of percussion instruments in Symphony Hall, there is a real live antique Underwood typewriter, with a metal plate installed in it to magnify the sound of the keys hitting the platen.

When the Pops performs this piece, they do a "shtick" with one of the percussionists coming out in the front of the stage and acting like a great visiting guest soloist. The stagehands make a big deal about setting up the typewriter "just so." The percussionist who is going to play the typewriter makes a grand entrance, and puts on an old fashioned green visor. Then he stuffs an oversized plastic cigar in his mouth, to look like an old fashioned newsroom reporter.

Before I continue, let me tell you about yet another interesting cultural difference in Japan. On many busy city street intersections, they have pedestrian overpasses so you don't have to wait for traffic to stop. And on the railings of all these overpasses, stuck on with double sided tape, there are thousands and thousands of little postcard-sized advertisements for, well . . . shall we say, ladies of the night. There were many different versions of these little advertisements. They were all very neatly attached to the railings in overlapping rows, each with a different picture of a young lady, with modesty just

153

barely satisfied by a strategically placed phone number.

Well, being Americans, we started to collect these things, and pretty soon we were trading them like baseball cards.

Anyway, back in the concert hall, we were all ready to play *The Typewriter*. The percussionist had gone through his entire shtick of getting the cigar and the visor. The Japanese audience had continued to observe all of this in total silence, failing to see any of the humor in it. Just when we were ready to start playing, the percussionist opened his music, and there, taped in the middle of his part (where only the orchestra could see it) was one of these little hooker handouts.

The percussionist tried desperately to hide this thing but it was too late—we all saw it, and in the midst of this solemn silence, we all burst out laughing.

The audience had no clue. They must have thought we were crazy.

*   *   *

One night we were going to play a show a hundred miles outside of Tokyo, so we hopped on one of the bullet trains and were there in about 45 minutes. We had left Tokyo at 5:00 p.m., so when we got there we needed to get some dinner. We looked around, but for some reason we just couldn't find any restaurants.

After much walking (and with time running out), we saw a place that had a little flag out front. This flag was similar to the flags we had seen in front of many Tokyo restaurants, so we opened the door and walked in. This was one *small* restaurant . . . just two tables, so our little party of six crowded in as best we could.

A lady came out to greet us, with repeated bowing. At this point, we tried to order some dinner with our non-existent Japanese. After a while she started to bring out some little items to eat, which, quite frankly, were pretty slim pickings. Then we noticed this woman giving her teenage daughter some instructions. The daughter went out, and five minutes later she came back with a big bowl of rice for us.

Now at this point, we were starting to wonder: Is this really a restaurant? Or did we just walk into someone's house and demand to be fed? Japanese people are so polite, it was really hard to know for sure.

It was a pretty basic little meal, and we all had the same thing. The entire time, we were the only ones there. After we ate, we paid a scribbled bill. To my dying day I will never know if that was a very unpopular and poorly run restaurant, or if we were home invaders.

This Time, with Feeling

When you play a musical instrument for a living, the job itself is all about emotional expression; no matter how "professional" you may be, you constantly feel emotionally vulnerable and exposed.

This feeling of vulnerability is at its height in the conductor-to-player relationship because, given the way orchestras work, conductors have all the power. They sit in judgment of your lifetime of developed skill. With such extreme imbalances of power at work, and with so much raw emotional energy so close to the surface, well, even in the best of relationships sparks occasionally fly.

There was one conductor I used to play for that always bothered me. He wasn't a bad person per se, and in retrospect I am grateful for his getting the money together to put on concerts and giving me a check so I could pay my rent that month. But he had a very bad managerial habit, which was, he really didn't seem to appreciate all the work we were doing for him. It wasn't any one thing, it was a lot of little things that added up, and well, I admit this was not very professional of me, but one night I just sort of "snapped," and I decided to play a little musical joke on this guy.

We were going to play a Mozart symphony that night, and before the concert I told a friend in the audience, "Pay attention to the slow movement. You're going to see something very unusual tonight."

For you civilians out there, a little bit of technical trivia: the principal bass player has enormous power over the rhythm of an ensemble, be it a jazz band or a symphony. In the *boom-chick-chick* or *oom-pah-pah* of music, the bass is the *boom* (or the *oom*), and for all the flash and glitter and supposed importance of the melody and the treble instruments, in the overall rhythmic structure, everyone else has to wait for the *boom* or the *oom*. By messing about with the placement of these *boom/oom* notes (i.e., playing a little ahead of the established beat or a little behind it), the bass player can easily alter the tempo for the entire ensemble, because the *chick-chick* or the *pah-pah* off-beats can only bounce off the "pulse" of the bass.

In this concert I was the principal bass player, which meant the other bass players had to follow me no matter what. So in the slow movement of this Mozart symphony, I started to play each downbeat just a *tiny* fraction of a second later on each bar. Sure enough, bit by bit, the tempo slowed down. I mean it really slowed down—to a crawl.

I have to tell you, I had no idea that my little scheme would be so successful. The whole exercise took on a life of its own. I became so fascinated and drugged with the power that I suddenly realized I had, that I couldn't help myself. I made the music go slower, and slower, and SLLoowweerrr . . . until I swear, it was like the whole thing was just hanging in midair.

There was nothing the conductor could do about it—although

I don't think he even noticed anything was wrong, which is one of the reasons why I had decided to do this to him in the first place. Finally I think it did occur to him that things were awfully slow, so he gave a huge heaving upbeat and we kind of had to get back on track, but right after that I just slowed it down again. Altogether I think I must have doubled the length of that slow movement.

I figured that was enough, I had made my point, so I let him do the last movement in regular tempo . . . with me leading, of course.

My friend in the audience knew something was going to happen, but he didn't know what. Being a professional musician himself, when the music started he knew right off what I was doing. But it was so subtle; there was no way for anyone else to know what had happened. My friend came up to me at intermission with tears streaming down his face. The poor guy, he had been in total hysterics through the whole thing but didn't dare laugh out loud.

The moral of the story? Always be nice to the bass player.

The View from the Pit

When you work as a professional freelance musician, one of the many occupational hazards you must face is playing in orchestra pits.

Most concerts are played in the relatively open space of a stage, and the orchestra is up above the audience. But in a pit, you're in a very small confined space, and you're way down below everything. In this windowless subterranean world, you are completely surrounded by barren walls, and all you can see of the theater above you is its ceiling—unless you are seated in the part of the pit that is directly underneath the stage itself, in which case you can't see anything. There is very little in the way of aesthetics in a typical orchestra pit—usually, the walls are just unpainted plaster or concrete. Then there's the dust. Gravity being what it is, all the dust, dirt, and desultory dramatic detritus of a theater tends to collect in its lowest point (i.e., the pit), and orchestra pits are rarely (if ever) cleaned, as doing so would require moving all the chairs and instruments out and then putting them all back in again. No one wants to do that, as it took forever to get everyone's chair crammed in there just exactly "so," so that everyone has enough room to play in the first place.

Playing in an orchestra pit is a unique study in sensory deprivation. Ballets are the worst in this regard, as they have no singing or dialogue. As you play *The Nutcracker* or *Sleeping Beauty* or *Giselle*, you know there is a show going on overhead, and you are very much a part of it, but you can't see it. You can hear the pitter-patter of anorexic little feet thumping on the stage above you, and you can hear the crowd laughing or applauding in the same places night after night, but you have no idea what it is they're laughing at or applauding for. You tell yourself that someday you're going hire a substitute, buy a ticket to the show, and come see just what the heck is going on . . . but you never do.

During an intermission, people in the audience always stand around the edge of the pit and look down at the orchestra. Since they are "up there" and you are "down here," there is a subtly implied class difference which makes any conversation with them feel somewhat awkward. So for the most part they would just stare at us and we would pretend not to notice them staring at us. Whenever that happened I always felt very much like I was a polar bear at the zoo.

Another big difference between playing concerts on stage and playing shows in orchestra pits is the repetition. The programs of symphony and pops programs change fairly regularly (sometimes every night), and operas and ballets tend to run for a few weeks at the most, but a Broadway show can run for years at a time. The big advantage of show work is that it is very steady employment. "Show" musicians are generally much more prosperous than the average freelance orchestra player, whose concert work is often sporadic and seasonal. The downside of show work, though, is that you have to play the exact same show, i.e., the exact same sequence of often painfully easy notes, night after night after night. The matinee

160

days are especially painful, because on those days you have to play the show twice. After a while it starts to feel like working in a factory. But at least in a factory, they occasionally re-tool. *Camelot* never changes.

Another big difference between playing concerts and playing shows is the dialogue. I once played part of the Boston run of *Annie* (this show would run for months, or even years, at a time), and that show has a lot of dialogue. You would play a song, then you had to wait five or ten minutes before you would play again. You couldn't just sit there and listen to the same dialogue every night, because if you did, after a while you would go insane. So the pit took on the appearance of a public library. There were books and magazines piled up everywhere. I only played a few weeks of that run, but some of the guys in that pit had been playing that same show, eight times a week, for two years. Those guys had to be the most literate group of show musicians ever. And what was most amazing to me was that, no matter how engrossed everyone may have been in their reading material, there was always a subconscious internal ear at work, listening for a line from the actors that would awaken them from their article in last June's *People Magazine*. Without any cuing, at the exact same moment, everyone would put down their reading material and pick up their instruments, just in time to play the next tune.

The Boston theater district includes the Opera House, the Wilbur, Schubert, and Colonial Theaters, and the Wang Center (a converted movie house with about 5,000 seats). These five venues are all inconveniently located within three blocks of each other, which means that parking at show time is almost impossible. I still have nightmares about not being able to find a parking space in the theater district as show time relentlessly ticks nearer and nearer. There were many times when I had to

161

park far away and shlep a bass six blocks, in my tuxedo, in the snow.

But in spite of all the dust, claustrophobia, repetition, and parking problems, oddly enough, once the curtain went up, I really enjoyed playing in the pit for Broadway shows. Musically speaking, playing the bass for a show is a lot different than concert work. First of all, you're the only bass, so you don't have to constantly match up with other bass players in a section; second, the way most show tunes are written, the bass has a very commanding part almost all the time. You're playing a lot of *boom-chick-boom-chick* rhythm (where the bass is the *boom* and the set drummer is playing the *chick* on a snare drum or closed hi-hat cymbal), so the bass becomes the rhythmic heartbeat of this whole grand production. The parts were easy to play, and to me anyway, it was musically rewarding and a lot of fun, especially when you're playing some really great tunes from classic musicals.

While most of the shows I played were "post-Broadway" runs, there is also a long-standing show business tradition that newly created shows will "preview" in Boston, typically for five weeks, before opening on Broadway. One year I was hired to play for the pre-Broadway run of *My One and Only*. This show eventually made it to Broadway, with Tommy Tune and Twiggy in the starring roles.

Since the great classic Broadway musicals are so much a part our culture, we tend to forget that these shows did not just pop out of a box. Long before they opened on Broadway, these shows were written, re-written, and then re-re-written; songs were added or deleted, and entire scenes were reworked during their out-of-town previews. This was also the case with *My One and Only*.

My One and Only started out (as I heard the story) with a few guys with money who wanted to produce a revival of the musical *Li'l Abner*. They hired a director, who proceeded to talk the backers into doing an entirely new show, with Gershwin music. This was all well and good until the backers saw the show opening night, at which point they fired the director and brought in a whole new creative team.

Of course at that point the orchestra, theater, and actors had all been hired, and contracts had been signed, and we had to get paid, show or no show. So we started to do this show night after night for five weeks, even though it was being completely re-worked after each performance. Almost every night we were asked to come at 6:00 p.m. to rehearse the latest changes. We got paid extra for that, of course, so we were happy to do it.

That show was especially fun to play because of the Gershwin music. Also, at one point in the show, "Honey" Coles, the well-known tap dancer, did a little rhythmic tap duet with the bass, where I would play a little solo and he would dance to it, echoing the rhythm I played. Sometimes I would throw in tiny little rhythmic variations and he would always catch it. It's little things like that that can make your night.

Memories of playing Broadway shows tend to run all together, since each night is usually exactly the same as every other, but there was one night at *My One and Only* that was truly unforgettable.

In one part of the show, the main characters (played by Tommy Tune and Twiggy) were trying to escape from the bad guy, and they flew off to the Caribbean in their private plane. But the bad guy sabotaged the plane, so Tommy and Twiggy were forced down on a desert island. The next scene took place on the beach of this island. To create the beach effect in the scene, part of the stage floor was removed to expose a large steel basin. This held about a hundred gallons of water for the actors to splash around in.

This steel tank was in the center of the stage, at the downstage edge (i.e., near the audience). Every night, in order to keep the water from getting stagnant and stinky, the stagehands would empty the tank, and then they would fill it up again just before the next performance.

As per usual, we were all crammed into the pit, and as is typical in Broadway shows, the lone percussionist had a whole hardware store's worth of equipment around him. He had a big drum set, plus tympani, chimes, glockenspiel, xylophone, bass drum—the works. And all of this hardware was located dead center in the pit, under the overhang of the stage. In this case, directly under this water tank.

Well, one night we were going along playing the show the same as always, when I noticed out the corner of my eye that the percussionist was moving around in a way that was just not normal. He kept looking up and around, and it was kind of distracting. At one point I glanced over at him to see what was the matter, and in the faint glow of his stand light, I saw a little drop of water come down and . . . *plunk*. It landed right on his head.

He looked at me; he looked all around; then another drop of water—*plunk*—fell on his head again.

If you've ever seen *Journey to the Center of the Earth*, perhaps you recall that scene where James Mason chips a little piece of crystal off a wall, which starts a small leak that turns into a flood. If you have, you have some idea of what was about to happen in that pit.

Apparently, the stagehand who had emptied the tank the night before (or maybe the one who refilled it that day) had forgotten to replace the drain plug at the bottom of the tank. It had taken the entire first act for the water to soak its way through the plaster of the pit roof, but once it had soaked through, these droplets grew in intensity until it was a genuine downpour. And it didn't stop raining for the entire second act.

This meteorological phenomenon was limited to the space occupied by this percussionist. Everyone else was bone dry, but bit by bit, this guy and his tuxedo had become completely drenched. Sopping wet, utterly miserable, he played the whole second act in this indoor deluge. He tried to rig up a xylophone case as a poncho, but it didn't do much good, since he couldn't hold it in place while he was playing. His drums were all soaked, and everything made of wood was ruined. He had to occasionally tip his snare drum over to drain the water out, and when he hit the suspended cymbal, little droplets of water were sent up in the air, so much so that one could briefly see a rainbow in front of his stand light. Up above, Tommy Tune and Twiggy sang and danced the night away, while down in the pit we were all torn between genuine pity and hysterical laughter as we watched this poor guy doing his best to play the rest of the show in a monsoon.

It's not very often that you get caught in a downpour in an orchestra pit. But if you do, well, no matter—the show must go on.

A Long Night at the Opera

Early in my playing career, along with playing the Pops, I would often play for Sarah Caldwell's opera company. Working for Sarah was an experience unlike any other. She was a true dictator. She staged the operas, she conducted the orchestra, she chose the artists, and she even designed the security procedures.

Sarah had her peculiarities, and since orchestral musicians are creatures of habit, we often made fun of her unorthodox style of doing just about everything. But I will say this: when she did something, she did it whole hog. She rarely had enough money to fully execute her artistic visions, but at least she gave it her best shot (even if it was a long shot), every time. In the risk-averse world of classical music, I have learned to admire that.

One night, we were performing Beethoven's *Fidelio*. I won't go into the whole synopsis of the opera here. Suffice to say there's a woman named Leonore (although for the whole first act she is dressed like a man and calls herself Fidelio). She has a boyfriend. The boyfriend is imprisoned in a dungeon, and the bad guy plans to do the boyfriend in. Almost the entire second act takes place in this dungeon.

166

To magnify the effect of the dungeon's darkness, Sarah had decreed that each music stand in the orchestra pit would have two stand lights: one white light, for when we were above ground, and one blue light for when we were in the dungeon. These were turned on and off remotely by the stage crew.

Well, there we were in the Orpheum Theater in Boston, one of those fine old Boston institutions that have seen better days. There were three basses in this very shallow pit, which was not really a pit at all. We were clearly in view of the audience, even blocking the line of sight of the first 10 rows. To my right, Frank and Ralph were sharing the first music stand. I had my own music stand with its white and blue lights. To my left was the stage.

We played the first act without incident. Intermission went by, and when the curtain went up on Act II, up on the stage, about 15 feet away from me, was Jon Vickers (a terribly famous tenor), lying on a big black box, all chained up in this dungeon. Not that you could really see him . . . or in fact, very much of anything. This dungeon was dark. And I mean *dark*. It was so dark that once the audience intermission lights went down, it was a bit of a panic; it took a while for our pupils to dilate enough to be able to see the sheet music in the remaining dim blue light.

Okay, it was a dungeon, so it was dungeon music, you know, kinda creepy, noodle-ee-noodle-ee-NOODLE-EE-noodle-ee-noodle-ee-noodle-ee . . .

At this point Jon Vickers started to sing all about what a drag it is to be chained up in a dungeon. One would think this would be self-evident but it went on for quite a while.

Anyway, I was playing this noodle-ee-noodle-ee-noodle-ee dungeon music when I got . . . just a whiff . . . of *smoke.*

Now remember, this was an old theater, made mostly out of wood, and I started to get truly panicked. What if the crowd gets a whiff of this? Will I be trampled and burned to death? My mind was racing. Meanwhile, 15 feet away, Jon Vickers continued to complain about being in a dungeon.

Then I happened to notice that the smoke was coming . . . from *my* stand light. The blue filter on the bulb was starting to ignite.

Oh, brother. They never mentioned this in music school. Well, this was an emergency. Despite the professional musicians' credo of "keep playing no matter what," in the middle of this pianissimo dungeon music, I turned off my blue stand light. Louder than the rest of the orchestra, the switch went . . . CLICK.

I suddenly found myself in *total* darkness. I mean, that music stand was just *gone.* I was getting paid to play these notes but I couldn't see any of them. I tried to read off Frank and Ralph's stand but it was too dark, and they were too far away.

Now bear in mind, I was just 19 years old at the time and it was maybe my third professional playing job ever and well, I ignored Ralph's advice to not be a hero. I decided to try and somehow recover. I figured, okay, the blue light is on fire. Let's use the white light.

CLICK.

Nothing. Then I realized that of course, there was no power to the white lights now. Okay, I thought, I'll just switch the bulbs.

Meanwhile, Jon Vickers is *still* singing away, and Frank and Ralph and the rest of the orchestra are *still* going noodle-ee-noodle-ee-noodle-ee-noodle-ee.

I started to unscrew the blue bulb. Ooh! ooh! ow! ow! . . . it was still hot.

So I unscrewed the white bulb first. Over this pianissimo music, in the near total darkness, you could easily hear the sound of a bulb being slowly unscrewed. SCRREE . . . SCRREE . . . SCRREE . . .

Okay, so that bulb was unscrewed. Then I unscrewed the blue bulb. I screwed the white bulb into the blue light fixture. Okay, let's get back in this opera. I threw the switch. CLICK.

!!
WHITE LIGHT
!!

Suddenly the brightest thing in the entire theater was the third chair bass player in the pit. I was blinded by the light. I shut it off. CLICK.

Jon Vickers *still* continued to sing about his unpleasant living conditions, while the rest of the orchestra, in near total darkness, still played noodle-ee-noodle-ee-noodle-ee-noodle-ee. I was starting to feel really left out.

At this point I just happened to look behind me, and there, on a banister of the shallow pit, I could barely make out the outlines of . . . spare bulbs! And there was a spare *blue* bulb!

169

Hooray! All was not lost.

So I screwed a blue bulb into the empty socket where I had unscrewed the white bulb. SCRREE . . . SCRREE . . . SCRREE . . .

I threw the switch.

CLICK.

Nothing.

Then, I remembered that this fixture had no power to it. Well I couldn't screw or unscrew any more bulbs; the stress of trying to keep the squealing to a minimum was just too much. So I had a brainstorm: I would switch the stand light's plug into a hot socket.

At this point I was trying to hold my bass up with one hand while I was feeling around in the total blackness of the disgusting sticky floor of this orchestra pit for the electrical socket where the plugs were.

I actually managed to find it, although my bass nearly fell over in the process.

Okay, let's get this going.

CLICK.

Nothing.

CLICK, CLICK.

Nothing, nothing.

I didn't figure out until later that the replacement blue bulb I had just screwed in . . . was burned out. I assumed I had plugged it into a dead socket.

So I spent the rest of the dungeon scene trying various plugs, all to no avail. Finally, Don Fernando and the cavalry showed up and saved everyone, including me, by bringing everyone outside. The stage lights came up enough that I could finally read my music. There was one page of music left in the opera.

What a night.

It turns out that this performance was recorded, and was just recently released on the VAI label. The liner notes say it was "a blazing performance." At last, a review I can agree with.

     *   *   *

One day at the Boston Ballet, we were rehearsing Tchaikovsky's *Sleeping Beauty* ballet.   At one point in rehearsal we were about to arrive at the big climactic statement of the main love theme.   We were cranking away on this constantly rising chromatic scale, and we were just about to play the big melody when the conductor, in a very excited and passionate voice, yelled out, "Violins! Sing!!! SING!!!!"

There were all these old guys playing violin in the orchestra. On hearing this instruction from the conductor, they all nodded their heads, put their violins in their laps and, five octaves lower than Tchaikovsky intended, sang:

"Deeee, daaaa, daaaaa . . ."

A Captive Audience

An eccentric philanthropist millionaire once gave me some money to fund the presentation of chamber music concerts (i.e., concerts featuring small ensembles like string quartets, quintets, etc.) . . . in prisons.

One does not normally associate convicted felons with Mozart string quartets, but grant money is grant money, and there it was. So I contacted some people in the state "corrections" department, and we scheduled a series of chamber music concerts for the inmates at some minimum and medium security facilities.

I tried very hard to come up with some very fancy artistic name for this nascent performing arts ensemble, but I needn't have bothered. The musicians that I hired to play the concerts immediately dubbed it "The Gas Chamber Players," and that's what everyone called it from then on.

While I admit I was little intimidated going into a prison for the first time, I am very glad I had the experience. It's beyond the scope of this one chapter to discuss policies of the penal system, but given how many people are behind bars in the United States, how much it costs to keep them there, and the fact that most of them are eventually going to be released, I think every citizen should endeavor to become more informed about the subject. I guarantee you, if you ever visit a prison, you will never think about phrases like "tough on crime" the same way again. When I walked in there I thought I was going to see a lot of "bad guys," but instead I saw a lot of human beings, not that much different from myself, coping with very difficult circumstances.

It was really quite interesting to play for these audiences. Before doing these events, I had never really realized that when you play a classical music concert, you have this huge advantage (or maybe disadvantage) because you're usually playing for an audience that already knows the piece you're playing. Being aware of everyone in the audience "already knowing the piece" can really influence a performance. But with this audience, most of them had never heard a string sextet before, so every concert of Mozart or Brahms felt like we were playing a world premiere. Also, the "hoity-toity-ness" that is so often a part of the classical music business was completely absent at these events, and as a result, the energy of the players and the music was really wonderful.

One night we were playing in a minimum security facility. Such facilities have no bars or cells, but even so, the guards asked us (as a security formality), to open our instrument cases. Cellos, of course, have long metal endpins sticking out the bottom, and every cellist has to keep the end of their endpin sharp so they can stick it into a wooden floor and not have it slip out from under them. So as we were opening all the cases for the security guard, the cello player opened his case, and, with a big "clangedy-clang-clang," onto the prison's concrete floor fell a 14-inch metal file.

Look, Kids, Now He's De-Composing

One event generally dreaded by orchestral musicians everywhere is the inevitable . . . "Kiddie Koncert."

Everyone wants the kids to have fun and carry a lasting impression that orchestras are fun and wonderful, but the thing is, being in the audience for a symphony concert by definition requires sitting very still and making no sound for an hour or more at a time. For children, having to sit so still for so long a time can actually be psychologically painful. In many households, it is used as a form of punishment. Therefore, symphony concerts and children are not the best combination.

I played a lot of children's concerts in my playing days. Some of them were very good. But I am very sorry to report that others were not. Part of the problem is, symphony orchestras just aren't in that line of work, and the economics of orchestra concerts being what they are, there is usually little or no money in the budget to do a big visually-engaging event for a concert hall filled with bussed-in school children. So out of sheer financial necessity, some of the orchestras I played in would just do a one-hour version of an adult concert, with the assistant conductor giving a little lecture on some fine musicological point. The players would always just try to get through it while ignoring the buzz of distracted noise in the crowd, and everyone would just hope that the audience was somehow, despite their general lack of interest, soaking up a cultural experience.

Sad to say, I was bored out of my mind at more than one kiddie concert, but I at least had something to do. I genuinely pitied the kids in the audience at some of these concerts.

There was one time we were going to do a kiddie concert at the Boston Ballet. We were in the Wang Center, and so we had 5,000 high school kids in the seats. For every hundred kids there was maybe one teacher on guard duty—whatever it was, it wasn't enough. It was during the school day, so attendance was mandatory for everyone, and for this audience we were going to perform the entire *Sleeping Beauty* ballet. Three hours. No lecture. No changes from the regular show. Here goes.

Well, other than the usual drone of chit chat in the audience, this went along okay for the first act. But then, at intermission, someone in management decided to make a little extra money by opening the concession stand to all these kids. Not necessarily a bad idea, but the trouble was, when the audience came back for Act II, they were all armed with M&M's. Eventually, some whiz kid in a box seat way up in the second balcony made the necessary trigonometric calculations required to land an M&M right on top of the tympani heads in the orchestra pit. With its sugar-coated mass multiplied by its gravity-induced velocity, each M&M made a very satisfying "boing" noise with every accurate hit. Once the kids had the range, they fired for effect. Down they came. Boing, boing, boing.

*   *   *

Fortunately, the mind tends to block out truly unpleasant memories, so I don't remember a lot of the less-than-stellar children's concerts I played. But there is one I cannot forget—it was so traumatic I can never get it out of my mind.

We were playing in one of those old, all-purpose civic-center war memorial auditoriums, better used for wrestling matches. It had a big overhanging balcony all around, and the orchestra wasn't on the stage, we were out in the center of the floor. This meant we were completely surrounded; there was nowhere to retreat in case of a massive frontal assault. The conductor had come up with a real toe-tapping theme for this concert: it was called "Minuets Through the Ages." (No, I am not kidding.) We proceeded to play various Haydn and Mozart minuets, and in between each one, this conductor would turn around to these 8,000 hormone-soaked seventh graders and give them a little lecture on some obscure musicological point regarding 3/4 time.

Well, you would think that somehow, somewhere, *somebody* would have taken a look at this idea and realized that this would *not* hold the attention of a bunch of screaming seventh graders for 60 minutes, but . . . they didn't. So we started to play, and this guy would occasionally turn around and talk over the rumble; the kids became more and more hostile as the show went on. About halfway through, we completely lost them. We could barely hear ourselves playing over the talking. And, since the kids held the high ground of the balcony, we were pretty much doomed from the get-go. At one point, spitballs made out of the printed programs started to come raining down in a blizzard. In retrospect, I consider myself lucky to have gotten out of there alive.

*   *   *

Whenever I played a less-than-wonderful kiddie concert, it always bothered me for a more practical reason: deep in my narcissistic heart, I knew that my future livelihood as a musician was highly dependent upon effective audience development, and I hated to see opportunities to achieve that goal go to waste.

One fateful day I was hired to play a concert for children that included a lot of dancing, so we figured all right, at least there's something to look at, this should hold the kids' attention. But alas, the story was not terribly interesting, and eventually everyone, including the orchestra, just about fell asleep. That was bad enough, but in the middle of the show (and no, I am not making this up), six little kids came out carrying a stretcher with a body on it. They were supposed to be the pall bearers at Mozart's funeral.

I'm all for grand dramatic effects whenever appropriate, but gee whiz . . . Mozart's corpse? In a show designed for five year olds? I thought it was a bit much.

After playing this show about six times, I finally went up to the people producing the event and expressed my dismay. "Mozart's corpse?" I said. "Come on, guys. Surely you could do better than that. I mean, I'm just a lowly bass player, and even *I* could come up with something better than *that*."

"Well," they replied, "you're so smart, let's see you do it."

So I went home and pondered this little gauntlet thrown down at my creativity. The challenge was to create a 60-minute show that, for budgetary reasons, could use no more than four actors.

It had to use music from the standard (public domain) orchestra literature. And it had to work for all age groups—including 3, 5, 7, and 13-year olds, as well as their parents. And it had to actually teach something about music. Yikes.

I thought about this for quite a while. One night I was trying to come up with some kind of comedic court case based on one of the classic fairy tales, when I just blurted out the phrase, "Peter VS. the Wolf." At last, the Wolf would have his day in court.

As part of my research, I sat down with a lawyer and told him the original story of *Peter and the Wolf.* The first thing he said was, "Well, it's obvious the Wolf was denied due process," and we were off and running. The result was a courtroom comedy based on the characters and events of the original Prokofiev story. The musicians would each be called to the stand to be cross-examined by the Wolf, and all of the instruments would be demonstrated and explained in the process.

This show was a remarkable success at its premiere. Amazingly, it worked for kids of all ages, *and* their parents. Once *Peter VS. the Wolf* was produced in Massachusetts, I wondered if anyone else would want to do it. And maybe pay me money for the use of it? So I sent a few flyers around. Imagine my shock when the Phoenix Symphony scheduled it!

That was the beginning of a remarkable series of events. Some unknown musician who played the show in one distant city would call their cousin in another city to tell them about it, and bit by bit I started to get calls from orchestra managers from all over, asking about it and wanting to perform it.

This went on for several years, until one fine day I received an email from someone in, of all places, Brazil. They told me they wished to perform my "Pedro Versus O Lobo." They went on to say they were going to perform it in the "municipal theater" of Rio de Janeiro. Well I must admit, this didn't sound very classy– I had this vision of the local "municipal theater" as being one of those multi-purpose facilities with kids making ash trays at one end and a basketball hoop at the other. But Rio is Rio, so I asked them, "Well, would you be willing to fly me down and put me up?" "Sure," they said.

Well, ash trays and screaming kids or no, a free trip to Rio is nothing to sneeze at, so off I went. At one point I started to wonder if this would turn out to be one of those Nigerian email scams, but I had grown up listening to Antonio Carlos Jobim and Joao Gilberto singing about girls from Ipanema, and my curiosity was too much, so I took the chance.

Well . . . it turns out the "municipal theater," that is, *O Theatro Municipal do Rio de Janeiro*, is more or less the Carnegie Hall of South America. The entire building was imported from Europe back at the height of the rubber boom, it's loosely copied from the Paris Opera House, and it is one of the most beautiful edifices anywhere. The sets and costumes of the production rivaled those of a Broadway show, and local heartthrob soap opera stars were cast in the leading roles. There were 12 sold-out performances, and they put me up in a five-star hotel right on the beach.

The show is now catching on in Germany, it was recently done in Australia (in both English and Chinese), and it just had a premiere in The Bahamas.

When *Peter VS. the Wolf* is done in some exotic locale I am occasionally treated to a free flight and hotel to go see it. I have to say, traveling the world to see something of your own

180

being magnificently staged and performed for appreciative audiences is one of the biggest thrills anyone could ask for.

And I owe it all to Mozart's corpse.

[Editor's note: you can read the entire text of Peter VS.
the Wolf *(or a companion piece in the same genre,* The Phantom of the Orchestra*) on the author's website,* www.justinlocke.com.*]*

Keeping Score

A televised Pops concert has the same glamor and energy as a live Pops concert, only times 10. The lights are brighter, the schedule is tighter, the stars are bigger, and the pressure is higher.

As was so often the case in my life, I fell into working on Pops TV shows purely by accident.

For many years, the Pops Fourth of July shows and the Holiday Pops specials were produced by Boston's Channel 5, the local ABC affiliate. It just so happened that the operations manager for Channel 5 was a member of my health club. He found out from someone at the club that I was a bass player in the Pops and also worked as a video producer. So he walked up to me in the locker room one day, introduced himself, and said, "Hey, we're doing a TV show of the Pops and we need a score reader. You interested?"

"What the hell is a score reader?" I asked.

"Don't worry about it, just show up," he said.

"Fine," I said.

Well, the first thing I learned about score reading was, the score reader gets to sit "in the truck." A TV production truck contains about seven million dollars' worth of equipment. It is hauled around the country as a semi tractor trailer, and it very neatly contains an entire mobile broadcast production facility, including various tape decks, video switchers, audio mixing boards, 12 or more cameras, miles of cable, and its own engineer. When a big football or basketball game is broadcast, the stadium doesn't have all that equipment. The networks don't own it either—at least, not as many as they need. Instead, when covering a large live event, the networks very often rent one of these trucks.

The truck has three main compartments: "Video," which is a room filled with video tape recorders; "Audio," a complete sound studio packed into a phone booth; and "Production." The production room has three rows of seats, which all face a wall that has something like 40 television monitors on it. Above these smaller monitors are two large monitors: "Preview," which shows the shot we are planning to go to next, and "Program," which shows what's going out on the air right now. The director sits dead center in the front, where he has the best view of the shots coming from all 12 (or more) cameras. The score reader sits next to the director. Seated on the other side of the director is the technical director, who operates the switcher board, which is a huge bank of buttons and knobs that allow him to cut to, or dissolve between, the various camera shots.

The second row of seats is taken up by the producer, the assistant director, and the Chyron operator. (The Chyron is a computer that generates on-screen text.) In the third row, the muckety-mucks observe the whole operation.

Even before the show starts, a Pops TV production is a wonder in and of itself. Once one of these big production trucks is parked at the stage door of Symphony Hall, a few hundred yards of audio and video cables are shoved through a basement window, and all this black spaghetti is threaded up, up, up, around and all through Symphony Hall to all the cameras and microphones, wherever they may be: on the stage, in the balconies, in the lobbies, and on the main floor. Some of these cameras are mounted on "jibs," a long pole that operates a little like a teeter-totter, allowing the camera to float up and down. Some camera jibs are mounted on stationary tripods, up in the balconies. Other jibs are mounted on a trolley, and this trolley runs on a little railroad track that is placed across the front of the stage—it takes a three-man crew to operate it. Then there are usually at least three or four camera operators on the stage, who will either use tripods, or more often, will go "hand held." (The on-stage camera operators all wear rented tuxedos so they will be less noticeable.)

Just setting up the cameras can be a scheduling nightmare because in the holiday season, Symphony Hall is busy with rehearsals and concerts from 10 a.m. to 10 p.m. every day. You can't very well have camera guys running cable during a concert, so they work a graveyard shift.

Along with additional lighting, a Pops TV production calls for microphones. There are microphones everywhere: on stands, hanging from the ceiling, clipped to lapels of hosts and guests, and glued to the sides of soloists' faces. There is also an endless adjustment of the microphones to get them in a spot where they will pick up the sound of the oboe but not block the conductor's face. Something you've probably never realized (at least, I never did), is that when a camera gets a close-up of a player in the orchestra during the program, the audio engineer actually "pots up" the microphone of that player to make them sound louder in the sound mix—so not only are you seeing them close up, you are hearing them close up. It's all part of the magic of television.

So you may yet be wondering, as I once was, what the hell is a score reader?

As one might imagine, a score reader is someone who reads the score.[9] The way this all worked was, Bob Comiskey, the TV director I worked with all those years, would take the score and "block shots." That is, he would design the look of a performance by deciding which instruments would be on camera while a piece was being played. For example, right at the beginning, we might start with a shot of the conductor. Then on maybe the fourth bar, Bob would "take" to the first violin section, then on the eighth bar he might "take" to the brass section—and so on, building a sequence of shots all the way through to the end of the piece. These shots were all carefully planned as medium, wide, or close-ups, and specific cameras would be assigned to get each shot. Every single piece of music on the program would be blocked in this manner.

(Shots have to be precisely planned because there are lots of times when some musicians in an orchestra are not playing, and this is not very interesting to look at. Musicians also have a nasty habit of doing rather disgusting things with their instruments just before and after they play them. Spit valves

---

[9]The "score" is the sheet music used by the conductor. It shows all the notes of all the instruments. Scores are very dense, the notes are very small, and while you are reading them you have to turn a page every eight bars. Musicians in an orchestra don't read off a score; they only see a "part" that just has the notes for their instrument.

are not very attractive things to see in action, especially on network television.)

As the score reader, it was my job to tap my finger on the score in exact rhythmic sync with the orchestra, so Bob could glance down from the monitors, look at his markings in the score, and remind himself of exactly when to say "take." (On hearing the word "take," the "switcher" would hit a button, and the picture would switch to the next camera shot in the planned sequence; the TV audience at home would then see the shot change right on the beat.)

This task of tapping one's finger on the score in sync with the music may sound simple, and I guess it is. But it's not enough to just sit there and passively do that. A big part of the overall feel of the TV show is "taking" to the next shot at a precise point in time that makes rhythmic and musical sense. We always tried very hard to achieve this effect, and it got to the point where, instead of just tapping on the music, I was literally "conducting" Bob as he directed, giving him all the rhythmic information, cues, countdowns, preparatory beats, and verbal signals at just the right time before the take points.

As much fun as it was, there were many difficulties in doing that job. First of all, everyone in the truck is talking constantly—and occasionally yelling. And you're only hearing half of their conversations, because they're usually talking to someone on headset in Symphony Hall. This is very distracting when you're trying to listen to the music, especially in the quiet sections. Second, Bob was always busy looking at the monitors, so even though he pretty much had every shot memorized (he always astonished me in his ability to do this), I had to constantly look ahead to give him a sense of how much time he had before the next shot. And third, while on average we would "take" to a different camera every four to eight bars, sometimes there would be a shot on every bar—yikes.

Sometimes things would go awry—a camera would go dark and we'd have to wing it for a while, or a planned shot would be obscured by the scroll of a string bass, or, horror of horrors, we would just "get off" and find ourselves "taking" to shots of musicians pondering their stock portfolios and doing little else. If this happened I would have to read ahead (being careful not to lose my place) and tell everyone the number of the next shot coming up so we could all get back in sync. Over the years, we developed our own little coded language for special situations, like when Bob did a "take" early or late or skipped one altogether. I had no way of knowing if his departure from the plan was accidental or purposeful, so I would tell him that I had noticed, and I would say where we *ought* to be right now according to the plan in the score.

Another problem I faced in that job was the scores themselves. Many Pops arrangements were written long before there were computer music writing programs, which meant they were handwritten, and sometimes not very clearly. Some old Pops arrangements would have musical shorthand in them, like entire 16 bar repeats just written as mostly empty bars with little circled numbers referring to bars on another page. When I hit a spot like that I just had to hope and pray that I was in the right place because there were no notes to check my position against. Repeats were always a major difficulty, since they would have two layers of camera cues: one for the first time through, and another one 4 inches lower for the second time through. Eventually, I just always had the library make me a score that was "linear," so I wouldn't have to suddenly turn back three pages in the middle of a fast tune. And I would have to transfer all of Bob's numbers and notes to that version without making any errors.

The number one terror in that job was the possibility of getting lost. The places where getting lost was most likely were also those places where the choreography of the camera cuts was the most complex, so being off by one bar could mean that, instead of a great whiz-bang visual effect, there would be five shots in a row of musicians wiping rosin off their fingernails, or worse. When the cues were coming fast and furious like that in a live broadcast, as much as I enjoyed the excitement of it all, I often found myself longing for the halcyon days when I was a lowly bass player and there were six other guys who could take up the slack if I fell asleep. In that truck, I was on my own. The stress was absolutely enormous, far beyond even the stress of being in the orchestra. I eventually had to learn to go into a total Zen state before each show and completely clear my mind of anything and everything. I had to tune out that immense overload of information that was in the truck—not just the talking, but the video too. I had to keep my mind off the fact that a million people were tuned in *right now* and the precise rhythmic coordination of all these images was riding on my index finger. During the music, I could never risk looking up at the monitors even for a second, so I never saw the shows live—I always had to tape the broadcast and watch it afterwards at home.

There are a lot of times in Pops TV shows when the orchestra is not playing, and at those delightful moments I could just sit back and observe television being made. I could see all 12 camera monitors at once, and I could watch Bob do his director thing. While he was in total command of all the camera operators, he also had a team of "floor directors" in the hall who made his every wish come true without question. A TV director is very similar to what God must be like, because whatever Bob said instantly happened. For example, Bob would say, "Dim the lights," and the lights would dim. Then he would say, "Send him out," and like magic, the conductor would come out. Then he would say, "Applause applause applause"—and, via cues from the floor directors, the audience would start to applaud. "Mikes up and cue 'em," and the sound guys would turn up the hosts' microphones, the on-camera hosts would start talking, and I could see the teleprompter text going by as the hosts read it to the camera.

Seeing this dimension of live television production never ceased to amaze me. I always felt like I was watching the best show in town, from the best seat in the house.

*   *   *

Whenever we did a live broadcast of the Pops Fourth of July show, we always did a TV rehearsal the night before. Our "rehearsal" consisted of shooting the live concert on July 3rd. Since it was a live show, there was no going back for mistakes, and so it was always a bit of a crunch even in the best of circumstances.

One year though, we had a particularly bad July 3rd TV rehearsal. Everything that could go wrong did go wrong. After an unending series of broken cameras, shots that didn't work, headsets that didn't work, audio problems, and miscommunications with the stage crew and conductor, a very long night finally came to an end. As the audience's applause died down, all of us in the truck just sat there silently for a moment to catch our breath and collect ourselves.

Right at that moment, a familiar sound came over the truck's speaker system. Either by design or by accident, my old fan club had gathered around one of the microphones placed for picking up crowd noise, and the tiny little production room of the truck reverberated with the sound of 30 people yelling:

"All-right-Jus-tin!"

Everyone in the truck just stared at me. I didn't know how to begin to explain.

*   *   *

The first time I met Keith Lockhart was a few years after I had left the orchestra. I was in Symphony Hall, working with the TV crew, listening to the rehearsal for Keith's first Pops Fourth of July TV show. When the rehearsal ended, the musicians (as usual) bolted off the stage in about 10 seconds, and Keith was left on the podium all by himself. In a few moments a horde of symphony staffers would be surrounding him, but for the moment he was all alone. I thought, here's a golden opportunity: I will be bold and run up there and introduce myself and maybe pitch my *Peter VS. the Wolf* program to him while I'm at it. So with some trepidation I went up to him and said, "Mr. Lockhart, how do you do, my name is Justin Locke." I was sort of expecting him to say, "Nice to meet you" and walk away, but instead he said (and I am not making this up):

"THE Justin Locke? Author of *Peter VS. the Wolf?*"

I was totally shocked at this response. It turned out that Keith had conducted a performance of *Peter VS. the Wolf* way back when he was the assistant conductor of the Akron Symphony. At this point a bunch of administrative people had come out to the podium to talk to Keith, but he just ignored them and kept on talking to me. We had a lovely conversation as he told me how much he enjoyed doing the show. Sad to say, to date I've never been able to get the Pops to do it, but anyway . . . .

Six months later I was again working on a Pops TV show. This time it was Keith's first Holiday Pops TV taping. After the show, Keith and all the BSO brass came out to the production truck to meet all the TV production brass. In this very small truck space, all the introductions were going around between all these very highly ranked TV muckety-mucks and all the BSO

191

muckety-mucks, until the only person not yet introduced was . . . me.

I could tell that the TV people weren't exactly sure if I was important enough to get introduced to Keith, because in my role as the score reader, I was essentially just a glorified technician. Also, I had just recently left the Pops, and in orchestra culture the only thing lower than a bass player is an *ex*-bass player, so I also lacked any real status in the eyes of the BSO brass; I could sense that they were not terribly eager to introduce me to Keith either. At this moment there was a short, but extremely awkward, pause.

Keith broke this momentary silence. He put out his hand and said, "Justin! How are ya??"

I have to say, this was a wonderful moment. On the faces of all my TV friends, I could see a very impressed: "Oh my god! He knows Keith!"

And on the faces of the BSO brass, I could see:

"Oh my god. He knows Keith."

Apotheosis

In the hour preceding a Pops concert at Symphony Hall, there is an ever-crescendoing buzz of excitement backstage. All around you there are bits and pieces of the event that is slowly coming to life. In various nooks and crannies and in the "tuning room" stage right, you can see individual instrumentalists in their tuxedos and formal gowns practicing little passages from the music on that night's program. You can feel the tension and excitement relentlessly building as concert time creeps ever closer, and it is always amusing to see that energy reflected in the wide-open eyes of guests who have made it that far into the inner sanctum.

That backstage excitement is wonderful, but it is nothing compared to what lies through the looking glass of the stage entrance itself. When you cross that threshold, you find yourself transported into another world altogether, where the lights are shining brightly and, over the rumble of the 2,000 people in the audience, you hear one of the most famous orchestras in the world warming up. What's more, all that sound is reverberating throughout the acoustical marvel that is Symphony Hall. Once upon a time, I was able to walk out into that magical world and be, not a passive observer, but an actual participant in the grand fairy tale that is playing in a great orchestra. There are few experiences in life that can compare to it.

Being allowed to play in professional orchestras was a tremendous gift. While the job was often tedious and always very stressful, very often it was also just wonderfully exciting. It gave me a sense of personal, professional, and artistic validation that, at age 20 I took for granted, but have now come to understand is a very rare thing. Playing for millions of adoring fans and traveling the world with all expenses paid was as much fun as it sounds, and I hope that by reading this book, you have been able to share a little bit of that grand adventure with me.

So that leads me to the two questions people always ask me about my music career: How could I ever give it up? And do I miss it?

Well, as you now know, there is a lot more to playing in an orchestra than what is immediately visible to the audience. The stress of the job is enormous, having to work nights and weekends is not always fun, and like any other job, no matter how glamorous it may be and no matter how much it pays per hour, sometimes you just get to a point where you realize you have faced every challenge, and it's time to move on.

But there are some things I do miss about that kind of work. Mostly, in a brave new corporate world of constantly shifting deadlines and approximate delivery times, I miss the professional musician's credo of "we are going to play this piece starting at eight o'clock sharp, and once we start we are not going to stop until we get to the very end, and no excuses."

But more than anything else, I think I miss the feeling of *belonging* that is unique to professional orchestral musicians. The best part of that can only be felt on stage while the music is being played, but I still own a small piece of it. Whenever I see my old cohorts, I see a light of acceptance in their eyes. Through their recognition, I am made to feel that I am still a bona fide, if now only honorary, member of our exclusive little club.

I have to say, the whole experience was so heady and intense that sometimes I have trouble comprehending just how an Ohio farm boy like myself ever managed to be allowed to play in orchestras like the Boston Pops in the first place. Starting out with little more than a borrowed plywood bass, a how-to book, and a bus ticket to Boston, I had the privilege of making a spiritual journey on a road that is very much sought after, yet is so much less traveled by. This Shakespearian quote seems all too appropriate: "If this were played on a stage now, I could condemn it as an improbable fiction." It all seems so terribly unlikely, that when I walk past one of the downtown Boston theaters, or when I drive past Boston's Hatch Shell or Symphony Hall, I often get the feeling that I just imagined the whole thing, and I was never really there at all.

Well . . . it isn't *quite* like I was never there. The little bass section "spin spot" in the Pops arrangement of *Seventy-Six Trombones* is probably still being observed from time to time. And 50 years from now, perhaps some young bass player who is yet unborn will get a laugh out of one of my slightly risqué title changes in the Pops sheet music. And my luggage tag from the Mancini tour is prominently displayed on my refrigerator door—I smile every time I see it.

There is one final thing: If you ever find yourself walking down Boston's Esplanade on some hot July evening, and you come by the Hatch Shell at the end of a Pops concert, take a moment to listen very carefully. When the applause dies down, amidst the low rumble of the musicians leaving the stage and the audience packing up their blankets and coolers, every once in a while, you can still hear the distant voices of 30 sun-stroked people in the front row, yelling out:

"All-right-Jus-tin!"

Real Men Don't Rehearse © 2005 Justin Locke

Justin Locke is a unique and entertaining speaker. For more information about his speaking appearances, as well as his family concerts and books, please visit the Justin Locke Productions Web site at

www.justinlocke.com